Seize the Day!

安河内哲也
a.k.a. **Ted Eguchi**
Illustration: **芹沢直樹**
Plot: **吉野敬介**

多読のすすめ

楽しめば楽しむほど、英語は読めるようになる!

　「英文多読シリーズ」は、読み出すと止まらない、ワクワクストーリーで、英語を読むことを純粋に楽しむためのものです。皆さんは、これを読み始めると、きっとストーリーの世界にハマってしまうでしょう。

　授業や参考書で精読を学び、それを繰り返し復習するのも大切な勉強です。しかし、それだけでは英文に触れる量が絶対的に不足してしまいます。ただ机で「勉強」しているだけでは、言語の修得に必要な反射神経がなかなか身に付かないのです。

　そこで、たくさんの英語に触れ、慣れるための、「多読」が必要になります。「多読」の秘訣は、勉強ではなく純粋に読書として英文を楽しむことです。

　日本語の読解も、勉強して覚えたわけではありませんよね。マンガや小説など、大好きな本を読みながら覚えたはずです。この小説は、難しい単語や構文を極力使わずに、シンプルな英語で読みやすく書かれています。でも、本当に大切な単語や熟語、構文はしっかり文の中に組み込んであります。

　「多読」のためには……
①普段勉強しているレベルより簡単であること
②内容が楽しく、興味が持てるものであること
③辞書を引いて調べることによって、読書が中断されないようにすること

　この三つが大切です。また、従来の多読教材では、「内容は簡単だけれど、語彙や表現のレベルが高すぎて読書が止まってしまう。」「内容が日本人にとっていまいち興味が持てない。」という声がよく聞かれました。

そこで、このシリーズでは以下の工夫をしました。
◎語彙のレベルや文法のレベルを制約して、おおむね英検準2級〜センター基礎レベルの英語で、オリジナルストーリーとして書き起こした。
◎日本人、特に若者にとって興味が持てる内容を題材とした。イラストを随所にちりばめ読みやすくし、一度読み出すと止められなくなる工夫をした。
◎単語が気になる場合でも、すぐに解決できる語句注を充実させた。
◎朗読音声を無料でダウンロードできるようにし、耳からもストーリーが楽しめるようにした。(英語・日本語・日英対訳)
◎一冊分のストーリーの長さを5,000〜6,000語程度とし、ある程度読み応えはあるが、長過ぎて嫌にならないところでストーリーを完結させた。
(本書は約6,600語で構成されている)

http://www.toshin.com/books/
※音声ダウンロードの際は、下記のパスワードが必要です。
詳細は上記のサイトをご参照ください。
ID: **eibuntadoku**　Password: **ikirodaiki**

このような学習効果を、綿密に計算してこのシリーズは作成されています。とは言っても、何より多読では、勉強のことを忘れて、純粋に楽しむことが重要です。いつでも、どこでも読んで読んで読みまくることによって、知らず知らずのうちに試験の英文も読めるようになってしまう。そんな人がたくさん生まれることを願っています。

英語だけで楽しむもよし、訳や単語・熟語の注釈を見ながら楽しむもよし、朗読を聞いて楽しむのもよし。最後まで、約6,600語の冒険の旅へと出かけましょう。

安河内哲也 a.k.a. Ted Eguchi

CONTENTS

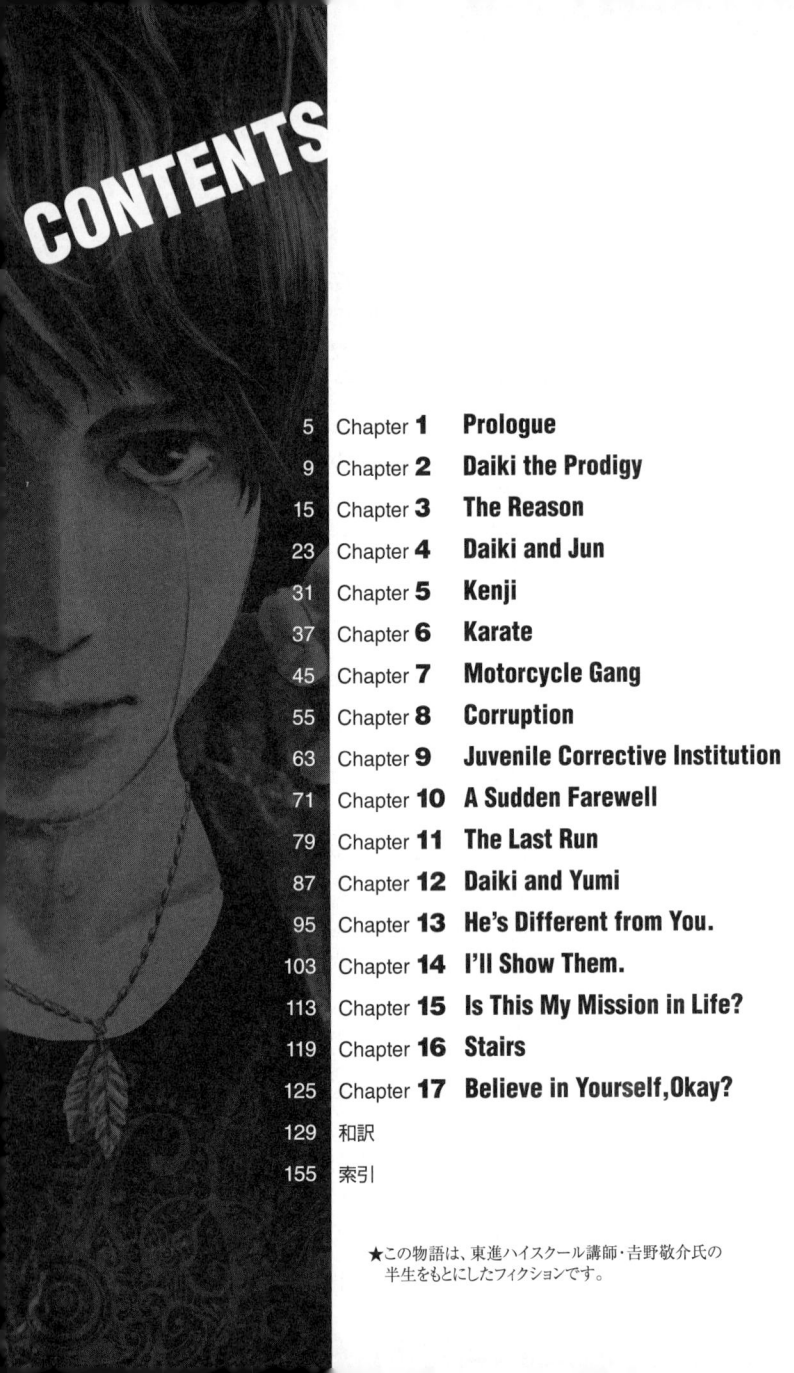

5	Chapter **1**	**Prologue**
9	Chapter **2**	**Daiki the Prodigy**
15	Chapter **3**	**The Reason**
23	Chapter **4**	**Daiki and Jun**
31	Chapter **5**	**Kenji**
37	Chapter **6**	**Karate**
45	Chapter **7**	**Motorcycle Gang**
55	Chapter **8**	**Corruption**
63	Chapter **9**	**Juvenile Corrective Institution**
71	Chapter **10**	**A Sudden Farewell**
79	Chapter **11**	**The Last Run**
87	Chapter **12**	**Daiki and Yumi**
95	Chapter **13**	**He's Different from You.**
103	Chapter **14**	**I'll Show Them.**
113	Chapter **15**	**Is This My Mission in Life?**
119	Chapter **16**	**Stairs**
125	Chapter **17**	**Believe in Yourself, Okay?**
129	和訳	
155	索引	

★この物語は、東進ハイスクール講師・吉野敬介氏の
半生をもとにしたフィクションです。

Seize the Day!

Chapter 1

Prologue

Seize the Day! — Prologue

This is a work of fiction inspired by a true story.

Prologue

Daiki Okuda teaches Japanese literature to students preparing for the entrance exams of prestigious universities. He is one of the top prep school teachers in Japan. He teaches in Tokushin seminar, one of the biggest and most prestigious prep schools in Japan. He also has his own juku, or privately owned cram school. He has written dozens

WORD LIST

work	名作品、著作
fiction	名小説、作り話
inspire	動引き起こす
Japanese literature	熟日本文学
prepare for ～	熟～に備える、準備する
entrance exam	熟入学試験
prestigious	形一流の、有名な
university	名大学
prep school	熟予備校
biggest	形 big の最上級
also	副～もまた、さらに
own	形自分自身の
juku	名塾
privately	副個人として
own	動所有する
cram school	熟塾、予備校
dozens of ～	熟多数の～

of books, which are very popular among students and adults alike.

"So, guys, listen carefully. You're never fools, even if sometimes you think you are. If you don't give up, you can achieve anything. Believe in yourself, okay?" he always says to his students. His words are very inspiring.

Many students, motivated by these words, have followed his methods, improved their scores dramatically and passed their entrance exams. Not

---

WORD LIST

□ popular	形 人気のある、評判の良い
□ among ~	前 ~の間で
□ alike	副 同様に
□ so	接 それでは、じゃあ
□ guy	名 〈呼びかけで〉君
□ carefully	副 注意深く、気を付けて
□ even if	熟 たとえ ..... でも
□ give up ~	熟 ~を諦める、止める
□ achieve	動 成し遂げる、達成する
□ believe in ~	熟 ~の価値を信じる
□ inspiring	形 人を鼓舞する
□ motivate	動 意欲を与える
□ follow	動 従う
□ method	名 方法論
□ improve	動 向上させる、進歩させる
□ score	名 点数、成績
□ dramatically	副 劇的に
□ pass	動 合格する、受かる

Seize the Day! Prologue

only that, many keep to these words even after they enter college and start to work. Many of them have achieved their goals and now work as doctors, lawyers and company managers.

Daiki has taught and nurtured many members of the elite, but he himself was not one of them.

This is the story of his life.

WORD LIST

- many　　　　　名多くのひと
- keep to ～　　熟～を固守する
- even　　　　　副～（で）さえ
- after　　　　　接～の後に（で）
- enter　　　　　動入学する
- college　　　　名大学
- start to V　　　熟Ｖし始める
- work　　　　　動働く、勤める
- achieve　　　　動成し遂げる、達成する
- goal　　　　　名目標、目的
- doctor　　　　名医師
- lawyer　　　　名弁護士
- company　　　名会社
- manager　　　名経営者
- nurture　　　　動育てる、教育する
- member　　　　名一員
- elite　　　　　名エリート、精鋭
- life　　　　　名人生

Seize the Day!

Chapter 2

Daiki the Prodigy

Daiki the Prodigy

Daiki Okuda was born in Ofuna, a suburb of Yokohama in 1966. He was brought up by kind, loving parents. His father worked in a bank and his mother sold life insurance. He had a brother named Seijiro, who was one year younger than Daiki. Daiki began to speak at a younger age than other kids and it was clear from the beginning that he was very smart.

WORD LIST

- prodigy　名天才児、神童
- be born　熟生まれる
- suburb　名郊外
- bring up ~　熟~を育てる
- work　動働く、勤める
- bank　名銀行
- life insurance　名生命保険
- name O C　熟OをCと名付ける
- younger　形 young の比較級
- than ~　接~よりも、~に比べて
- begin to V　熟Vし始める
- other　形その他の、別の
- kid　名子供
- be clear from the beginning　熟当初から明白である
- smart　形賢い、利口な

Chapter 2

In kindergarten, teachers often called him a prodigy. Daiki loved to be praised by teachers, so he often voluntarily cleaned the classroom or tidied up the books other kids had read and left behind.

In elementary school he did amazingly well in every subject, so it was natural that his parents decided to have him take the entrance exam for a prestigious junior high school. Daiki also took it for granted that he would pass.

In Japan, compulsory education lasts until the age

WORD LIST

- kindergarten ⑧幼稚園
- call O C ㊚OをCと呼ぶ
- praise ⑩褒める
- voluntarily ⑪自発的に
- tidy up ～ ㊚～を片付ける
- leave ～ behind ㊚～を置いて行く
- elementary school ㊚小学校
- amazingly ⑪驚くほど
- it is natural that ..... ㊚.....は当然である
- decide to V ㊚Vすることを決心する
- have O V ㊚OにVさせる
- take the entrance exam ㊚受験する
- prestigious ⑱一流の、有名な
- take it for granted that SV
  ㊚SがVすることを当然とみなす
- pass ⑩合格する、受かる
- compulsory education ㊚義務教育
- last ⑩続く

Seize the Day! Daiki the Prodigy

of fifteen and most students go to public schools until that age. However, some top students take entrance exams of prestigious junior high schools connected to high schools that send many students to top universities. This is what is called "an elite course."

In the fourth grade, he began going to a cram school and studying for the entrance exams. He did very well there, too. He had a rival named Makoto, who was in the same elementary school. Unlike

---

WORD LIST

- public school 熟公立学校
- take 動〈試験を〉を受ける
- entrance exam 熟入学試験
- prestigious 形一流の、有名な
- junior high school 熟中学校
- connected to ～ 熟～とつながった
- what is called 熟いわゆる
- elite 名エリート、精鋭
- grade 名学年
- cram school 熟塾、予備校
- rival 名競争相手
- elementary school 小学校
- unlike ～ 前～と違って

Daiki, who was a born genius and made the minimum effort to get good scores, Makoto devoted all his life to studying and barely kept up with Daiki. Daiki didn't worry very much about Makoto, but Makoto was very conscious of Daiki and how he did on the tests. Both of them were planning to take the examination of Koei Junior High School.

Months passed. The day finally arrived when the students who passed the entrance examination were to be announced at Koei Junior High School. It was a

---

WORD LIST

- born 形生まれながらの
- genius 名天才
- minimum 形最小限の
- make an effort 熟努力する
- score 名点数、成績
- devote A to B 熟 A を B にささげる
- barely 副なんとか、かろうじて
- keep up with 〜 熟〜に遅れずについて行く
- worry about 〜 熟〜を気にする
- be conscious of 〜 熟〜を意識している
- plan to V 熟 V するつもりである
- examination 名試験
- pass 動〈時が〉過ぎる、経つ
- finally 副ついに、ようやく
- arrive 動〈時が〉来る
- when ..... 接 ..... とき
- announce 動発表する

Seize the Day! **Daiki the Prodigy**

cold day. Daiki was waiting for the list to be posted. When it was finally put up on the board, Daiki looked for his ID number. It was as he had expected. He couldn't find his number.

[To be continued]

WORD LIST

- list ㊂表、名簿
- post ㊊はる
- put up ～ ㊋～を掲示する
- board ㊂掲示板
- look for ～ ㊋～を捜す
- ID number ㊋受験番号
- as ..... ㊈ ..... の通りに
- expect ㊊予想する
- find ㊊見つける

Chapter 3

The Reason

Seize the Day! The Reason

The Reason

Of course there was a reason for his failure.

Daiki had gotten a very bad cold just before the examination. Although he took medicine, his temperature was over 38 degrees Centigrade on the morning of the examination and the medicine was making him feel dizzy. He was in no condition to take the examination of a top school.

Daiki didn't want to just give up without trying, so

WORD LIST

- of course 熟 もちろん
- failure 名 失敗
- get a cold 熟 風邪を引く
- just 副 ちょうど
- although ..... 接 ..... にも関わらず
- take medicine 熟 薬を飲む
- temperature 名 体温、温度
- over 〜 前 〜以上
- 〜 degrees Centigrade 熟 セ氏〜度
- make O V 熟 O に V させる
- feel C 熟 C に感じる
- dizzy 形 目まいがする、ふらふらする
- be in no condition to V 熟 V できる状態ではない
- take 動 〈試験を〉受ける
- want to V 熟 V したいと思う
- give up 〜 熟 〜を諦める、止める
- without Ving 熟 V しないで、V せずに

Chapter 3

he went to take the test anyway. He was barely awake as he sat through the test. He couldn't do even half as well as he usually would have. After he got home, he went straight to bed and didn't wake up until two in the afternoon the next day.

When he learned he had failed the exam on the day of the announcement, he didn't make any excuses to his mother, who was with him. As Daiki and his mother were on their way home, they met Makoto and his mother.

WORD LIST

- so　接 だから
- anyway　副 ともかく
- barely　副 なんとか、かろうじて
- awake　形 眠らずに、目が覚めて
- as .....　接 ..... とき
- sit a test　熟 試験を受ける
- through ~　前 ~の間じゅう
- even　副 ~（で）さえ
- as well as A　熟 Aと同じくらい上手に
- get home　熟 家に帰る
- the next day　熟 翌日
- when .....　接 ..... とき
- fail　動〈試験に〉落ちる
- on the day of ~　熟 ~の日に
- announcement　名 発表、公表
- make an excuse　熟 言い訳をする
- be on one's way home　熟 家に帰る途中で

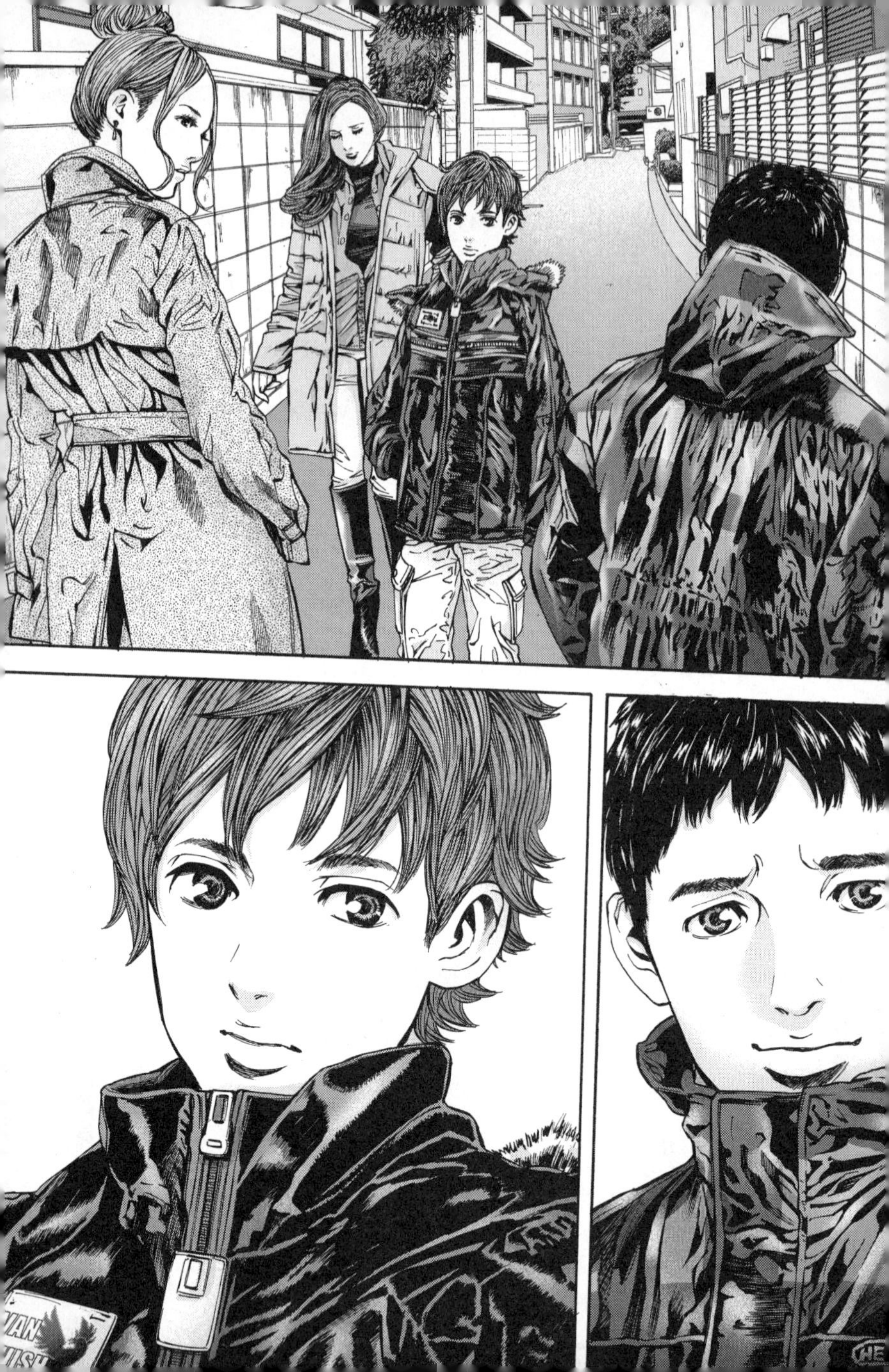

Chapter 3

Makoto said to Daiki, "Hi, Daiki. I did it. I passed. We're going to study at Koei together. Let's enjoy our new lives."

Daiki and his mother couldn't respond to his words but just nodded. An awkward silence lasted for a moment and Makoto instinctively knew that Daiki had failed and said, "Ah ... Sorry ... You might have ..."

"Don't worry. I just had bad luck. Congratulations, Makoto. Your efforts have finally paid off," Daiki

WORD LIST

- pass 動合格する、受かる
- respond to ~ 熟~に答える
- word 名言葉
- just 副かろうじて
- nod 動うなずく
- awkward 形ぎこちない
- last 動続く
- for a moment 熟少しの間
- instinctively 副直感的に
- Sorry 形すまなく思って
- might have Vpp 熟Vしてしまったかもしれない
- worry 動心配する
- luck 名運
- Congratulations 間おめでとう
- effort 名努力
- finally 副ついに、ようやく
- pay off 熟うまくいく

Seize the Day! The Reason

said, barely smiling.

"Oh, I'm very sorry. I think you'll be all right in the public school. With your intelligence, you can accomplish anything," Makoto said with a sympathetic look. However, despite Makoto's sad look, Daiki saw the corners of his lips were curled slightly upwards. Seeing that, Daiki felt more miserable than he had ever felt before. He couldn't help feeling how unfair the world was.

When Daiki got home, Seijiro was waiting for him.

WORD LIST

□ barely	副なんとか、かろうじて	□ curl	動ゆがめる
□ public school	熟公立学校	□ slightly	副わずかに
□ intelligence	名知能、知性	□ upwards	副上向きに
□ accomplish	動成し遂げる	□ feel C	動 C に感じる
□ sympathetic	形同情に満ちた	□ miserable	形惨めな
□ look	名顔つき、表情	□ cannot help Ving	熟 V せざるを得ない
□ however	副しかしながら	□ unfair	形不公平な
□ despite ~	前~にも関わらず	□ when	接 ..... とき
□ corner	名かど、片すみ	□ get home	熟家に帰る

Chapter 3

Seijiro knew Daiki had been feeling very bad on the day of the examination, so Seijiro didn't ask about the result. Seijiro just smiled and welcomed his brother home. Daiki smiled back and said, "Don't worry, bro. I'm all right. Say, how about a game of cards? Let's go upstairs," Seijiro smiled back, and the two went up to their room.

[To be continued]

WORD LIST

- on the day of ～ 熟 ～の日に
- examination 名 試験、テスト
- so 接 だから
- ask 動 尋ねる
- result 名 結果
- just ..... 副 ただ ..... だけ
- smile 動 微笑む
- welcome 動 喜んで迎える
- smile back 熟 微笑み返す
- worry 動 心配する
- bro 名 brother の略式
- say 動〈間投詞的に〉おい、そうだ
- how about ～? 熟 ～はどうですか？
- game of cards 熟 カードゲーム
- upstairs 副 2階へ
- go up to ～ 熟 ～の方へ行く

Seize the Day!

Chapter 4

Daiki and Jun

Daiki and Jun

And so, Daiki had to enter a public junior high school. He was very reluctant to attend the entrance ceremony. He didn't want to meet his friends from elementary school and explain to them that he had failed the entrance examination for Koei JHS. He didn't want to go to school at all because now he had no motivation to study anything. Daiki began to hate studying because he thought it was

WORD LIST

- and so 熟それで、だから
- have to V 熟Vしなければならない
- enter 動入学する
- public junior high school 熟公立中学校
- be reluctant to V 熟Vすることに気が進まない
- attend 動出席する
- entrance ceremony 熟入学式
- want to V 熟Vしたいと思う
- elementary school 熟小学校
- explain 動説明する
- fail 動〈試験に〉落ちる
- entrance examination 熟入学試験
- not ..... at all 熟少しも ..... ない
- because ..... 接 ..... なので
- motivation 名やる気、動機づけ
- begin to V 熟Vし始める
- hate Ving 熟Vすることを嫌う

Chapter 4

what had made him so miserable.

At the entrance ceremony he met many of his friends who didn't seem to care whether Daiki had failed the entrance examination or not.

Jun, an old friend of Daiki's, said, "Hey, I heard you failed. I'm sorry about that, but I'm actually happy because now I can hang out with you for three more years. To tell the truth, I was very sad because I thought I couldn't talk with you anymore."

Daiki was touched to hear that, and at the same

WORD LIST

□ so	副とても、非常に
□ miserable	形惨めな
□ many	名多くのひと
□ seem to V	熟Vするように思える
□ care	動気にする
□ whether	接SがVするかどうか
□ old	形昔なじみの
□ hear	動耳にする、聞いて知る
□ sorry	形残念に思って
□ actually	副実際に
□ hang out with ~	熟~とつるむ
□ more	形より以上の
□ to tell the truth	熟実を言えば
□ sad	形悲しい
□ talk with ~	熟~と話す
□ anymore	副もはや、これ以上
□ touch	動感動させる
□ at the same time	熟同時に

Seize the Day! Daiki and Jun

time he was ashamed that he had taken it for granted that he was going to leave Jun and many old friends. He now realized his friends were much more valuable than doing well in school.

Jun was a very tall boy with short curly hair. He had an impulsive personality and was very short-tempered. From the time he was very small, he was constantly getting into trouble. When he was angry, he was never able to control his temper.

After the entrance ceremony, Jun and Daiki were

WORD LIST

- ashamed ..... 形 ..... であることを恥じて
- take it for granted that SV 熟 SがVすることを当然とみなす
- leave 動去る、離れる
- realize 動理解する
- much 副ずっと
- valuable 形価値のある
- do well in school 熟学校で良い成績を取る
- curly hair 熟縮れ毛
- impulsive 形直情的な、衝動的な
- personality 名性格
- short-tempered 形短気な
- constantly 副いつも
- get into trouble 熟問題を起こす
- when ..... 接 ..... とき
- be able to V 熟Vすることができる
- control one's temper 熟怒りを抑える
- entrance ceremony 熟入学式

walking together to the school gate, when three boys surrounded them. They didn't look like first year students. All of them were tall.

"Hi. How are you guys doing? We're a little short of money. Would you guys like to help us out? Perhaps you could lend us some," the biggest guy said smiling, but his tone was very threatening. Daiki's heart started pounding. He didn't know what to do. He thought he had no choice but to pay some money to defuse the situation.

WORD LIST

- gate 名門
- surround 動囲む
- look like ~ 熟~のように見える
- first year student 熟一年生
- a little 熟少し、わずか
- be short of ~ 熟~が不足している
- Would you like to V? 熟Vしてくれませんか?
- help ~ out 熟~を手伝う
- perhaps 副できれば
- biggest 形 big の最上級
- tone 名口調
- threatening 形脅迫的な
- start Ving 熟 V し始める
- pound 動〈心臓が〉どきどきする
- have no choice but to V
  熟 V するよりほかにどうしようもない
- defuse 動静める
- situation 名状況

Seize the Day! Daiki and Jun

Before Daiki knew it, Jun was dashing toward the tallest boy. Then he leaned back clenching his fist and hit the boy with all his might. Jun caught the boy by surprise and hit him square in the face. The boy fell down, blood pouring from his nose. Then Jun began kicking him hard. The other two boys froze, unable to move. There was blood all over the ground. The boy sobbed and begged, saying, "Please stop. I'm sorry. I'm sorry," but Jun didn't stop until the boy finally passed out.

WORD LIST

☐ dash	動突進する	☐ begin Ving	熟Ⅴし始める
☐ toward ~	前~に向かって	☐ freeze	動凍り付く
☐ lean back	熟上体を後ろに反らす	☐ be unable to V	熟Ⅴすることができない
☐ clench	動固く握り締める	☐ all over ~	熟~のいたるところで
☐ fist	名握りこぶし	☐ sob	動泣きじゃくる
☐ catch ~ by surprise	熟~の不意を突く	☐ beg	動懇願する
☐ square	副まともに	☐ finally	副ついに、ようやく
☐ fall down	熟倒れる	☐ pass out	熟意識を失う
☐ pour	動流れ出る		

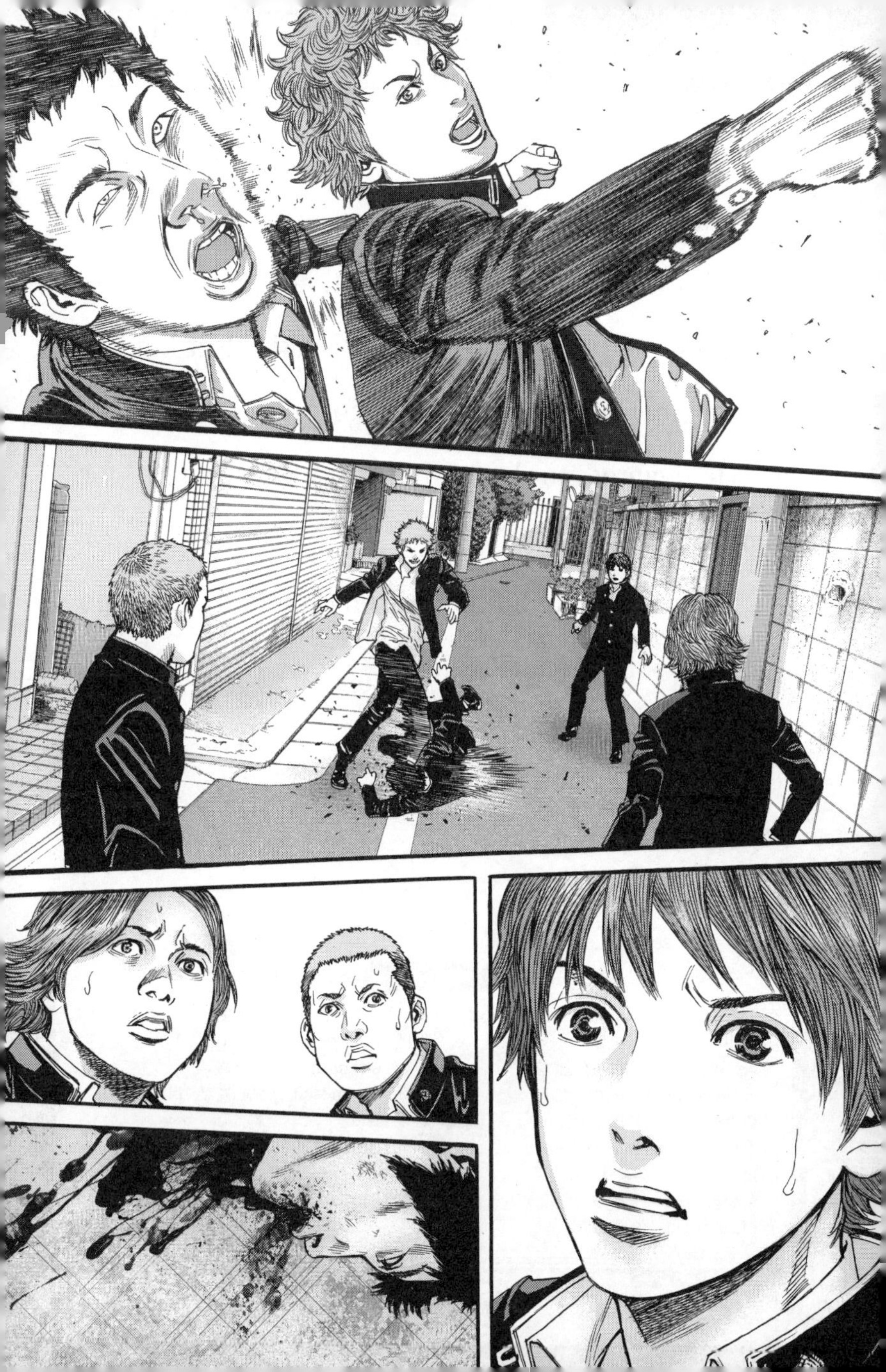

Seize the Day! Daiki and Jun

Daiki and the other two boys just stood looking. Daiki was a bit scared of Jun but, at the same time, he thought Jun was very cool. Daiki felt a kind of excitement he had never felt before.

He wanted to have that kind of strength for himself.

Later it turned out that the boy Jun had beaten up was the school gang leader.

[To be continued]

WORD LIST

- just ..... 剾ただ ..... だけ
- a bit 熟少し
- be scared of ～ 熟～を恐れる
- at the same time 熟同時に
- think 動思う
- cool 形かっこいい
- feel 動感じる、思う
- a kind of ～ 熟～のようなもの
- excitement 名興奮
- never ..... 剾一度も ..... ない
- before 剾以前に
- strength 名強さ
- for oneself 熟独力で、自分のために
- later 剾後で
- turn out that ..... 熟 ..... であることが判明する
- beat up ～ 熟～をぶちのめす
- school gang leader 熟学校の番長

Seize the Day!

Chapter 5

Kenji

Kenji

Daiki didn't study at all. Not even a little. He hated it. In class, he just slept or read comic books. Of course teachers sometimes scolded him, but he ignored them or just went out of the classroom to take a walk with Jun, who was in the same class. They were always together. They smoked cigarettes behind the school building and talked about the stories in the comic books they had been reading.

WORD LIST

☐ not ..... at all	熟少しも ..... ない	☐ scold	動叱る
☐ even	副〜（で）さえ	☐ ignore	動無視する
☐ a little	熟少し、わずか	☐ go out of 〜	熟〜から出て行く
☐ hate	動ひどく嫌う	☐ take a walk	熟散歩する
☐ class	名授業	☐ same	形同じ
☐ just	副ただ ..... だけ	☐ smoke a cigarette	熟タバコを吸う
☐ comic book	熟マンガ本	☐ behind 〜	前〜の後ろで
☐ of course	熟もちろん	☐ talk about 〜	熟〜について話す
☐ sometimes	副時々	☐ story	名物語

Chapter 5

Now Daiki and Jun were well known to all the teachers and students as the guys who had beaten up the school gang leader. Not many talked to them or cared about them. They could do almost anything they liked.

One year passed like that, and Daiki began to get bored. One day when Daiki and Jun were walking, they noticed that there was a Karate dojo near the school. It looked interesting, so they went in.

Several boys were practicing there. They looked

WORD LIST			
□ be well known to ~	熟~によく知られている	□ get C	熟 C になる
□ as ~	前~として	□ bored	形退屈した
□ beat up ~	熟~をぶちのめす	□ when	接 ..... とき
□ talk to ~	熟~に話しかける	□ notice	動気付く
□ care about ~	熟~を気にする	□ Karate dojo	熟空手道場
□ almost	副ほとんど	□ look C	熟 C に見える
□ pass	動〈時が〉過ぎる、経つ	□ interesting	形面白い
□ like ~	前~のように	□ several	形何人かの
□ begin to V	熟 V し始める	□ practice	動練習する

Seize the Day! Kenji

like high school and junior high school students. The sensei, or the teacher, was a man with a firm body. They were not fighting each other, but instead they were practicing katas, or forms. It looked like they were dancing. On seeing that, Daiki and Jun laughed. They laughed so loud that everybody there could hear them.

One boy stopped and said to them, "So you think this is funny, huh? This is not a place for weaklings like you. Go away." He was a short guy with short

WORD LIST

□ look like 〜	熟〜のように見える	□ on Ving	熟Ｖするとすぐに
□ high school	熟高校	□ laugh	動笑う
□ junior high school	熟中学校	□ so 〜 that S V	
□ firm	形引き締まった		熟とても〜なのでＳはＶする
□ fight	動格闘する、張り合う	□ loud	副大声で、うるさく
□ each other	熟お互い	□ hear	動耳にする
□ instead	副その代わりに	□ funny	形おかしい
□ kata	名空手の型	□ weakling	名弱虫
□ form	名フォーム、型	□ like 〜	前〜のような

Chapter 5

hair. He had a firm body just like his sensei.

Hearing that, Jun dashed toward him. Daiki thought Jun would beat up the boy as usual. Jun always knocked out his opponents with the first punch. Jun leaned backward as usual and sent his fist forward with all his might. Daiki thought, "This is it!"

But the boy easily dodged the punch, and chopped Jun's back. Jun fell and landed facedown on the floor. He got up, coughed, and again dashed toward the

---

WORD LIST

☐ dash	動突進する	☐ forward	副前へ
☐ toward ~	前~に向かって	☐ with all one's might	熟全力を尽くして
☐ beat up ~	熟~をぶちのめす	☐ easily	副容易に
☐ as usual	熟いつものように	☐ dodge	動かわす
☐ knock out ~	熟~を失神させる	☐ chop	動一撃を加える
☐ opponent	名敵、相手	☐ back	名背中
☐ lean	動傾く、もたれかかる	☐ land	動落ちる
☐ backward	副後ろ向きに、あおむけに	☐ facedown	副うつ伏せに
☐ fist	名握りこぶし	☐ cough	動咳をする

Seize the Day! Kenji

boy. This time the boy also dashed toward Jun, bent down and punched Jun hard in the stomach.

Jun fell rolling to the floor, panting, "I'll kill you …"

"Okay, do it if you can. Come on. Is that all you've got?" said the boy.

[To be continued]

WORD LIST

☐ toward 〜	㊤〜に向かって
☐ this time	㊤今度は
☐ also	㊤〜もまた、さらに
☐ bend down	㊤腰を低くする
☐ punch	㊤パンチをくらわす
☐ hard	㊤激しく、強く
☐ stomach	㊤腹部、胃
☐ fall	㊤倒れる
☐ roll	㊤転がる
☐ floor	㊤床
☐ pant	㊤あえぐ
☐ kill	㊤殺す
☐ if	㊤もし ..... ならば
☐ come on	㊤勝負しよう、さあ来い

Chapter 6

Karate

Seize the Day!

Karate

Jun got up, but he was staggering and unsteady. He raised his fist again. Just as he was about to throw another punch, the boy kicked him in the belly. Jun flew through the air for a moment and landed on the floor with a loud noise. He was knocked out.

Daiki stood in a daze, unable to say a word. The boy was much stronger than Jun, whom Daiki had thought to be the strongest boy around.

WORD LIST

☐ stagger	動よろめく	☐ fly through the air	熟空を切って飛ぶ
☐ unsteady	形不安定な	☐ for a moment	熟少しの間
☐ raise	動上げる	☐ land	動落ちる
☐ fist	名握りこぶし	☐ loud	形(音が) 大きい、うるさい
☐ as	接 ..... とき	☐ knock out ~	熟~を失神させる
☐ be about to V	熟まさにVしようとしている	☐ in a daze	熟ぼうっとして
☐ throw	動打つ、見舞わせる	☐ be unable to V	熟Vすることができない
☐ punch	名パンチ	☐ much	副ずっと
☐ belly	名腹部	☐ around	副近くに、周囲に

Chapter 6

"Hey, you! Help me get him up. Come on," said the boy to Daiki.

Daiki didn't say a word and helped him carry Jun to the corner. The sensei and other students were looking at them. The boy said to the sensei, "Can I take care of this guy for a while, Sensei?" The sensei nodded.

The boy put a pillow under Jun's head and asked Daiki to watch him. He went away and came back with a wet towel. When he put the towel on his

WORD LIST

□ help O V	熟 O が V するのを助ける
□ get ~ up	熟 ~を起こす
□ come on	熟 さあ行こう
□ carry	動 運ぶ
□ corner	名 かど、片すみ
□ look at ~	熟 ~を見る
□ take care of ~	熟 ~の面倒を見る
□ guy	名 奴、男
□ for a while	熟 しばらく
□ nod	動 うなずく
□ pillow	名 枕
□ ask 人 to V	熟 人に V するように頼む
□ go away	熟 立ち去る
□ come back	熟 戻る
□ wet	形 濡れた
□ towel	名 タオル
□ when	接 ..... とき

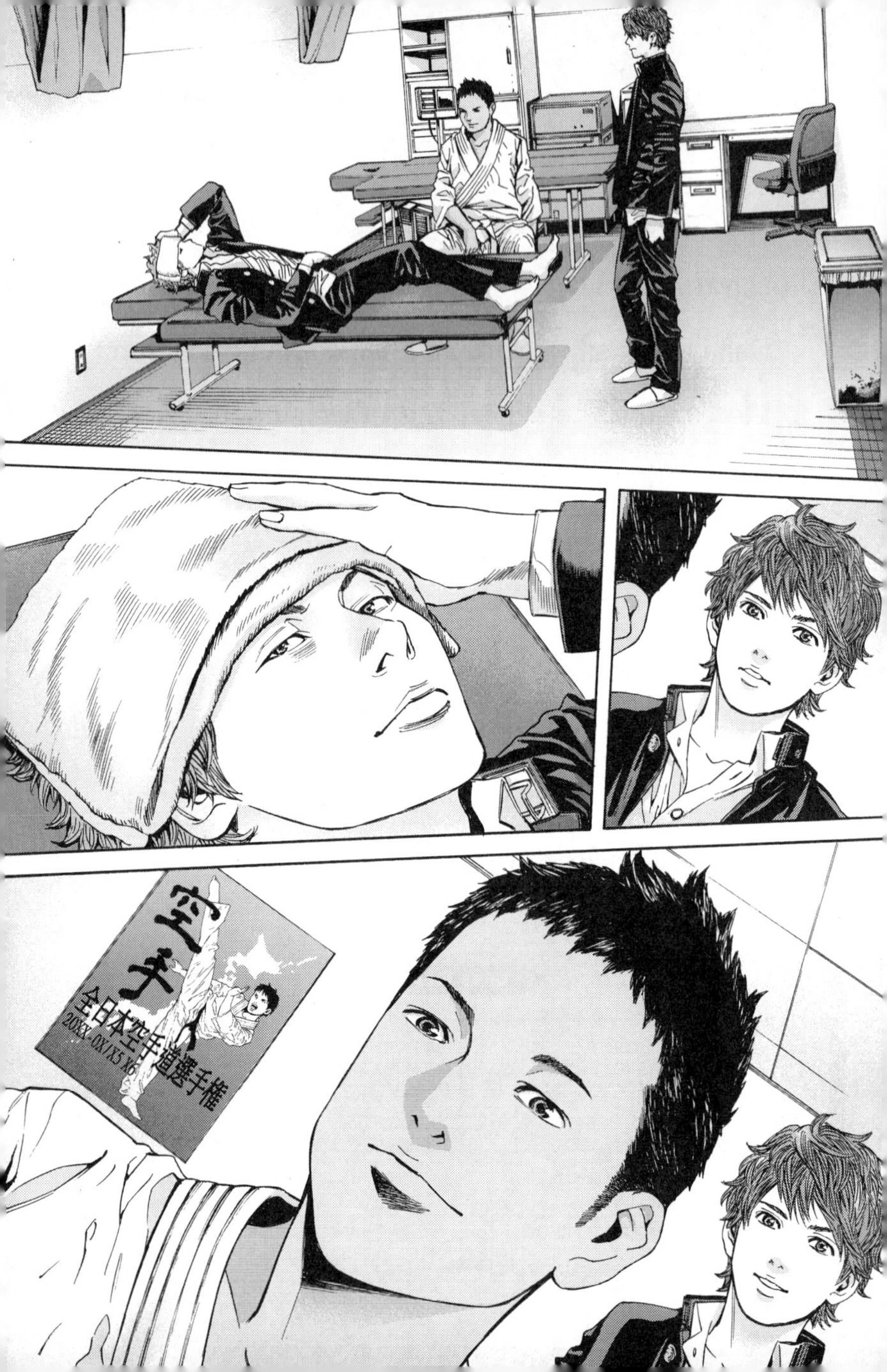
空手
全日本空手道選手権
20XX-0X/X5 X6

Chapter 6

forehead, Jun opened his eyes. The look of anger was gone.

The boy said to Jun, "We had a good fight, right? With your power, you can be a great karate fighter. You should learn karate here." Without saying a word, Jun nodded.

"What's your name?" asked Daiki.

"Kenji. Kenji Okura. Just call me Kenji."

When they got talking, the sensei said to them angrily, "What are you guys doing? Kenji, get back to

---

WORD LIST

☐ forehead	名額	☐ word	名言葉
☐ look of anger	熟怒った顔つき	☐ nod	動うなずく
☐ gone	形なくなった	☐ ask	動尋ねる
☐ fight	名戦い、格闘	☐ call O C	熟OをCと呼ぶ
☐ with 〜	前〜があれば	☐ when	接.....とき
☐ power	名力	☐ get Ving	熟Vし始める
☐ karate	名空手	☐ angrily	副怒って
☐ fighter	名戦う人	☐ guy	名〈呼びかけで〉君
☐ without Ving	熟Vしないで、Vせずに	☐ get back to 〜	熟〜に戻る

Seize the Day! Karate

practice. And you two, if you want to join, change into dogis. There are some spare ones in the locker room."

This is how Daiki and Jun started to learn karate. Kenji was in the same grade in junior high school as Daiki and Jun.

After the practice, Daiki, Jun and Kenji went out of the dojo. Then they found a big black sedan with tinted windows parked in front of the dojo. A man like a yakuza, with dark glasses, was behind the

WORD LIST

- practice ㊂練習、けいこ
- join ㊙加わる
- change into ～ ㊚～に着替える
- dogi ㊂道着
- spare ㊠予備の
- locker room ㊚更衣室
- start to V ㊚V し始める
- grade ㊂学年
- junior high school ㊚中学校
- go out of ～ ㊚～から出て行く
- sedan ㊂セダン型自動車
- tinted ㊠色の付いた
- park ㊙駐車させる
- in front of ～ ㊚～の前に
- like ～ ㊙～のような
- dark glasses ㊚サングラス
- behind the wheel ㊚〈車を〉運転して
- look at ～ ㊚～を見る

Chapter 6

wheel and was looking at them.

[To be continued]

Seize the Day!

Chapter 7

Motorcycle Gang

Seize the Day! Motorcycle Gang

Motorcycle Gang

Kenji said to the man, "Hey, bro, thank you for picking me up. These are my new friends, Jun and Daiki."

"All right guys, hop in," Kenji's brother said, and the three of them climbed into the back seat. The engine roared and rock'n'roll music played loudly. Daiki and Jun thought the man and the car were very cool.

WORD LIST

- motorcycle gang 熟暴走族
- bro 名 brother の略式
- thank you for Ving
  熟 V してくれてありがとう
- pick ~ up 熟〜を車で迎えに来る
- guy 名〈呼びかけで〉君
- hop in 熟跳び乗る
- climb into ~ 熟〜に乗り込む
- back seat 熟後部座席
- engine 名エンジン
- roar 動うなる
- rock'n'roll music 熟ロックの音楽
- play 動〈音楽が〉演奏される
- loudly 副大声で、うるさく
- think 動思う
- cool 形かっこいい

Chapter 7

Daiki and Jun didn't study at all and didn't belong to any clubs, so karate was the only thing they learned. They went to the dojo every day and worked very diligently. They wanted to be strong – as strong as Kenji.

One and a half years passed. Daiki, Jun, and Kenji were always together. Now the three of them were the best karate fighters in the city. They had had numerous fights and beaten up a lot of delinquents in the area. Now their names were known throughout

WORD LIST	
☐ not ..... at all	熟 少しも ..... ない
☐ belong to ~	熟 ～に所属する
☐ club	名 クラブ
☐ so	接 だから
☐ dojo	名 道場
☐ work	動 練習する
☐ diligently	副 精を出して
☐ as A as B	熟 Bと同じほどA
☐ pass	動〈時が〉過ぎる、経つ
☐ best	形 最も上手な
☐ fighter	名 戦う人
☐ numerous	形 数多くの
☐ fight	名 戦い、格闘
☐ beat up ~	熟 ～をぶちのめす
☐ a lot of ~	熟 たくさんの～
☐ delinquent	名 不良
☐ area	名 地元
☐ throughout ~	前 ～のいたるところに

Seize the Day! Motorcycle Gang

the Yokohama area.

Kenji went to a different junior high and like Daiki and Jun, he didn't study, either. Now the three of them had to decide which high school to go on to, but they only had one choice, Seikai High School. It was a very unpopular private school that would accept anyone, so many juvenile delinquents went on to this school.

The three of them entered Seikai High. There also, they spent their days fighting numerous fights.

WORD LIST

- different 形違った
- junior high 熟中学校
- like ~ 前~のように
- either 副~もまた（~ない）
- decide 動決定する
- go on to ~ 熟~に進学する
- choice 名選択
- unpopular 形人気のない、不評の
- private school 熟私立の学校
- accept 動受け入れる
- anyone 代誰でも
- so 接だから
- juvenile delinquent 熟不良
- enter 動入学する
- also 副~もまた、さらに
- spend 時間 Ving 熟Vするのに時間を費やす
- fight 動格闘する、張り合う
- numerous 形数多くの

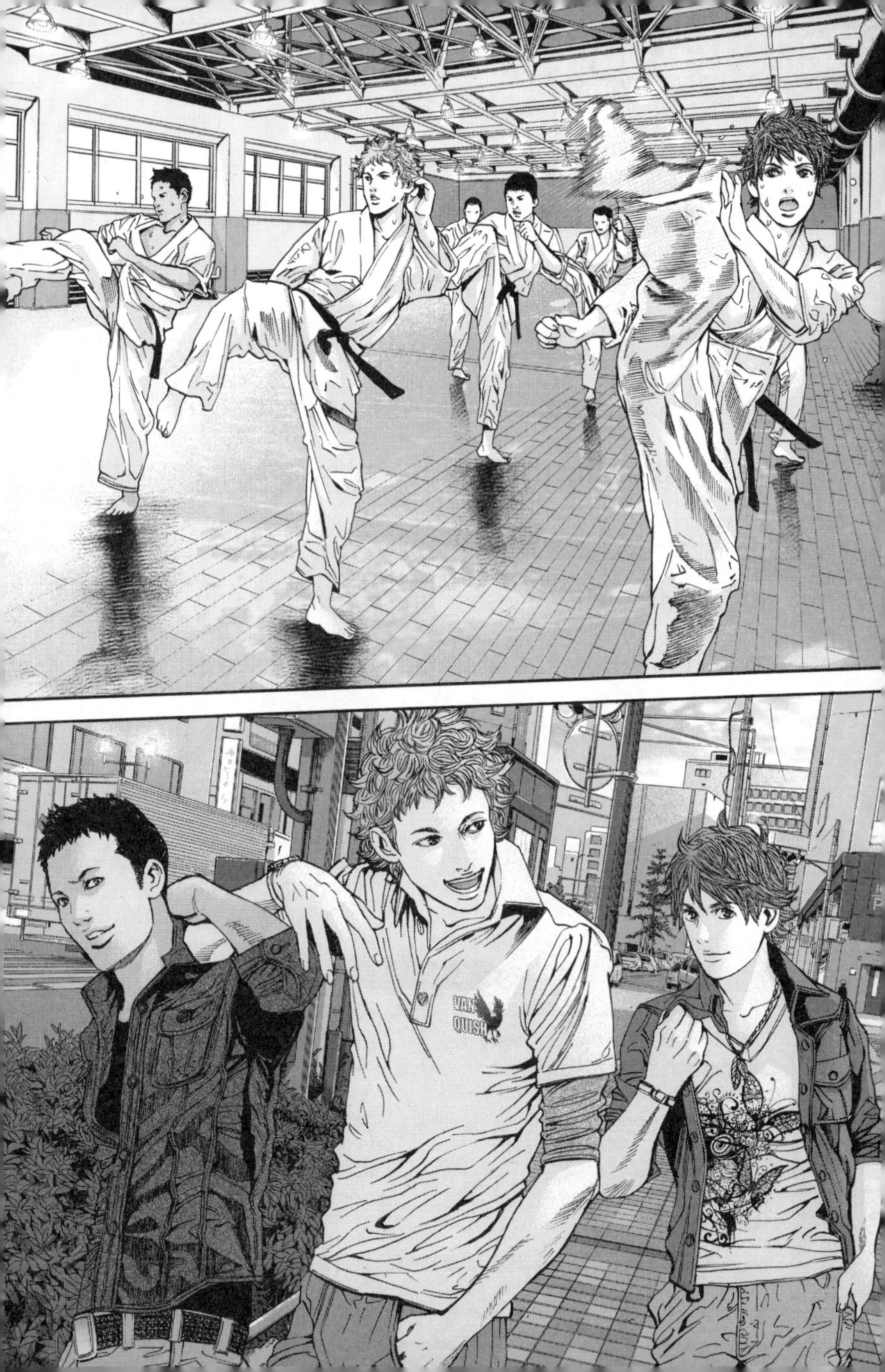
VAN
QUISH

Seize the Day! Motorcycle Gang

After they all turned sixteen, they decided to go to a driving school to get their motorcycle licenses. To get a license, in addition to the training, they had to attend many lectures and pass the final exam. If they were asleep in the classes, they couldn't get the credits. They wanted the license so much that they attended all the classes, but Jun and Kenji couldn't pass the final examination. Daiki passed the exam easily. He didn't prepare for the test, but his memory of the lectures had been enough for him to pass the

WORD LIST

- turn 動〜になる
- decide to V 熟Vすることを決心する
- driving school 熟自動車教習所
- motorcycle license 熟バイクの免許
- in addition to 〜 熟〜に加えて
- training 名運転の実習
- attend 動出席する
- lecture 名講義
- pass 動合格する、受かる
- asleep 形眠っている
- credit 名〈授業の〉単位
- much 副ずっと
- examination 名試験
- easily 副容易に
- prepare for 〜 熟〜に備える、準備する
- memory 名記憶
- enough for 〜 to V
  熟〜がVするのに十分な

test.

Jun and Kenji asked Daiki how to study for the test, so Daiki began teaching them. He taught them how to memorize information and how to solve questions – he had learned these techniques when he was preparing for the junior high school entrance examination.

They were impressed by Daiki's teaching skills. He was able to teach difficult concepts in easy-to-understand ways. He used examples and comparisons

---

WORD LIST

□ how to V	熟 Vする方法
□ so	接 だから
□ begin Ving	熟 Vし始める
□ memorize	動 暗記する
□ information	名 情報、知識
□ solve	動 解く
□ technique	名 技術、コツ
□ when	接 .....とき
□ junior high school	熟 中学校
□ entrance examination	熟 入学試験
□ impress	動 感動させる
□ skill	名 技術
□ be able to V	熟 Vできる
□ concept	名 概念
□ easy-to-understand	熟 理解しやすい
□ example	名 例
□ comparison	名 比喩

Seize the Day! Motorcycle Gang

they could relate to, and when they got bored, told jokes related to the topics. The next time, they passed the examination easily, thanks to Daiki. After they got their licenses, naturally they became members of the local motorcycle gang.

Members of motorcycle gangs used to customize their motorcycles with various ornaments and remove their mufflers in order to make their engines louder. They used to run together on the road so that everyone would notice them, a way for delinquent

WORD LIST

□ relate to ~	熟 ~を理解する
□ get C	熟 C になる
□ bored	形 退屈した
□ related to ~	熟 ~に関係のある
□ thanks to ~	熟 ~のおかげで
□ naturally	副 当然、自然に
□ become C	熟 C になる
□ used to V	熟 よく V したものだ
□ customize	動 カスタマイズする
□ various	形 さまざまな
□ ornament	名 飾り、装飾
□ remove	動 外す
□ muffler	名 (エンジンの) 消音器、マフラー
□ make O C	熟 O を C にする
□ loud	形 (音が) 大きい、うるさい
□ so that S will V	熟 S が V するように
□ notice	動 注目する
□ delinquent	形 怠惰な、非行の

Chapter 7

boys to get their existence recognized by the public.

Motorcycle gangs were a kind of juvenile delinquency that was quite common in the 70's and 80's in Japan. They were usually composed of boys aged sixteen to twenty and were quite well organized. Each gang had a strict hierarchy with each gang member having an individual role and class that was strictly observed.

One day, Daiki, Jun and Kenji were summoned by the gang leader. Usually when individual gang

---

WORD LIST

□ get ~ Vpp	熟~にVしてもらう、される	□ strict	形厳しい
□ existence	名存在	□ hierarchy	名階層制度、ヒエラルキー
□ recognize	動認める	□ individual	形個々の
□ the public	熟一般の人々	□ role	名役割
□ juvenile delinquency	熟不良行為	□ strictly	副厳格に
□ quite	副かなり	□ observe	動守る
□ common	形よく起こる、一般的な	□ summon	動呼び出す
□ be composed of ~	熟~から成り立つ	□ gang leader	熟暴走族の総長
□ organized	形組織化された		

Seize the Day! Motorcycle Gang

members were named and summoned, it was a very serious business. The three of them were asked to come to the harbor at midnight. Daiki wondered what it was about.

When they arrived at the harbor, some of the gang leaders asked them to stand on the edge of the waterfront. They lined up in a row, and suddenly a big black sedan came racing toward them.

[To be continued]

WORD LIST

- name　　　　動 指名する
- summon　　　動 呼び出す
- serious　　　 形 重大な
- business　　 名 用件
- ask 人 to V　 熟 人にVするように頼む
- harbor　　　 名 港
- midnight　　 名 真夜中
- wonder .....　動 ..... かなと思う
- arrive at ～　 熟 ～に到着する
- some　　　　代 いくらかの人々
- on the edge of ～　熟 ～の端に
- waterfront　名 海岸の土地、河岸
- line up　　　熟 一列に並ぶ
- in a row　　 熟 一列に
- suddenly　　副 突然
- sedan　　　 名 セダン型自動車
- come Ving　 熟 V しながらやってくる
- race toward ～　熟 ～に向かって突進する

Chapter 8

Corruption

Seize the Day!

Corruption

Daiki, Jun and Kenji stood on the edge of the waterfront, looking at the black sedan speeding at them. They didn't move. Their sensei had told them they should never flinch at their enemy and they kept to his teaching. The sedan stopped just in front of them with a screech and the leader of the gang came out of the car. He was a big stout guy with permed hair who was wearing a black jacket. He

---

WORD LIST

- corruption 名堕落
- on the edge of ~ 熟~の端に
- waterfront 名海岸の土地、河岸
- look at ~ 熟~を見る
- sedan 名セダン型自動車
- speed 動加速する
- flinch 動ひるむ
- enemy 名敵
- keep to ~ 熟~を固守する
- in front of ~ 熟~の前に
- screech 名(ブレーキの) キーという音
- gang 名暴走族
- come out of ~ 熟~から現れる
- stout 形かっぷくのよい
- guy 名奴、男
- permed 形パーマがかかっている
- jacket 名上着

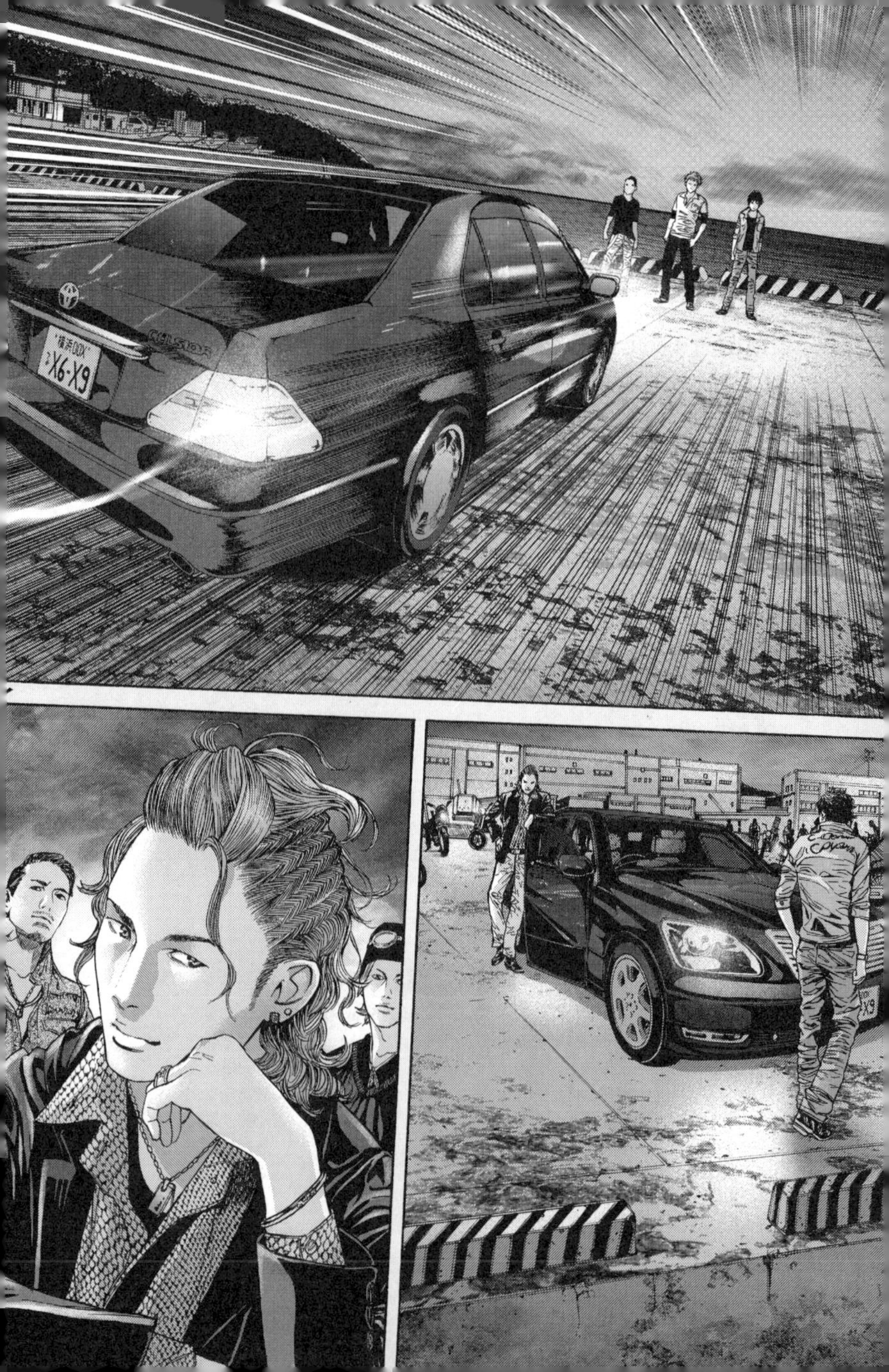
X6-X9

Seize the Day! Corruption

said, "All right. Well done. It seems that you have enough guts. Well, I heard you guys are great fighters. Now I want to assign you guys to important positions. You guys are going to be my bodyguards, all right?" This was exceptional. Being the leader's bodyguards meant they would be respected members of the gang. The three of them felt honored to be given the positions and they gladly accepted the offer.

Over the next several months, they experienced

WORD LIST

- Well done.　熟でかした、よくやった
- It seems that .....　熟 ..... であるらしい
- enough　形十分な
- gut　名根性、ガッツ
- hear　動耳にする
- assign　動任命する
- position　名地位
- bodyguard　名ボディーガード
- exceptional　形特別な
- mean　動意味する
- respected　形立派な
- feel honored　熟光栄に思う
- gladly　副喜んで
- accept　動受け入れる
- offer　名提案
- over ～　前～にわたって、～の間
- several　形いくつかの
- experience　動経験する

all the bad things that young guys could have imagined. They were at the prime of their lives. Daiki knew what they were doing was wrong but he couldn't control himself. After all, he was just going along with the other guys around him. He knew he was breaking many laws, but he didn't care. He thought it was adults and the unfairness of society that were wrong.

One evening he was playing cards with his brother, Seijiro, at home. Daiki could relax most when he was

WORD LIST

- all the ~　　熟すべての〜
- guy　　名奴、男
- imagine　　動想像する
- the prime of life　　熟人生の最盛期
- wrong　　形間違っている
- control oneself　　熟自制する
- after all　　熟結局
- just .....　　副ただ.....だけ
- go along with ~　　熟〜に同調する
- other　　形その他の、別の
- around ~　　前〜の周りに
- break　　動〈法律を〉犯す
- law　　名法律
- care　　動気にする
- unfairness　　名不公平さ
- society　　名社会
- play cards　　熟トランプをする

Seize the Day! Corruption

with Seijiro. Daiki was able to be himself when he was with his brother. Seijiro told Daiki about some girls he had met and asked him questions about sex that he could never have asked his father. Daiki had heard that brothers never got along, but he couldn't believe it. He thought he and Seijiro were the closest brothers in the world.

Suddenly they heard their mother calling them from downstairs. She said there were visitors for Daiki. Daiki went downstairs and saw two men in

WORD LIST

☐ be able to V	熟 Vすることができる	☐ believe	動信じる
☐ some	形いくらかの	☐ close	形親密な
☐ meet	動出会う	☐ suddenly	副突然
☐ ask	動尋ねる	☐ call	動呼ぶ
☐ question	名質問	☐ downstairs	名階下
☐ sex	名性	☐ visitor	名訪問者
☐ never	副決して〜ない		
☐ hear	動耳にする、聞いて知る		
☐ get along	熟仲良くやっていく		

Chapter 8

black suits. They said, "We have to take you to the police station for what you have done. We have all the evidence, so don't say anything and just come with us." Their mother was crying. Seijiro watched from the top of the stairs. His eyes were full of tears.

[To be continued]

WORD LIST

- suit　名スーツ
- have to V　熟Ｖしなければならない
- take 人 to ~　熟人を~へ連れて行く
- police station　熟警察署
- all the ~　熟すべての~
- evidence　名証拠
- so　接だから
- anything　代〈否定文で〉何も
- just .....　副ただ ..... だけ
- cry　動泣く
- watch　動見守る、見る
- the top of ~　熟~のてっぺん
- stairs　名階段
- eye　名目
- be full of ~　熟~でいっぱいである
- tear　名涙

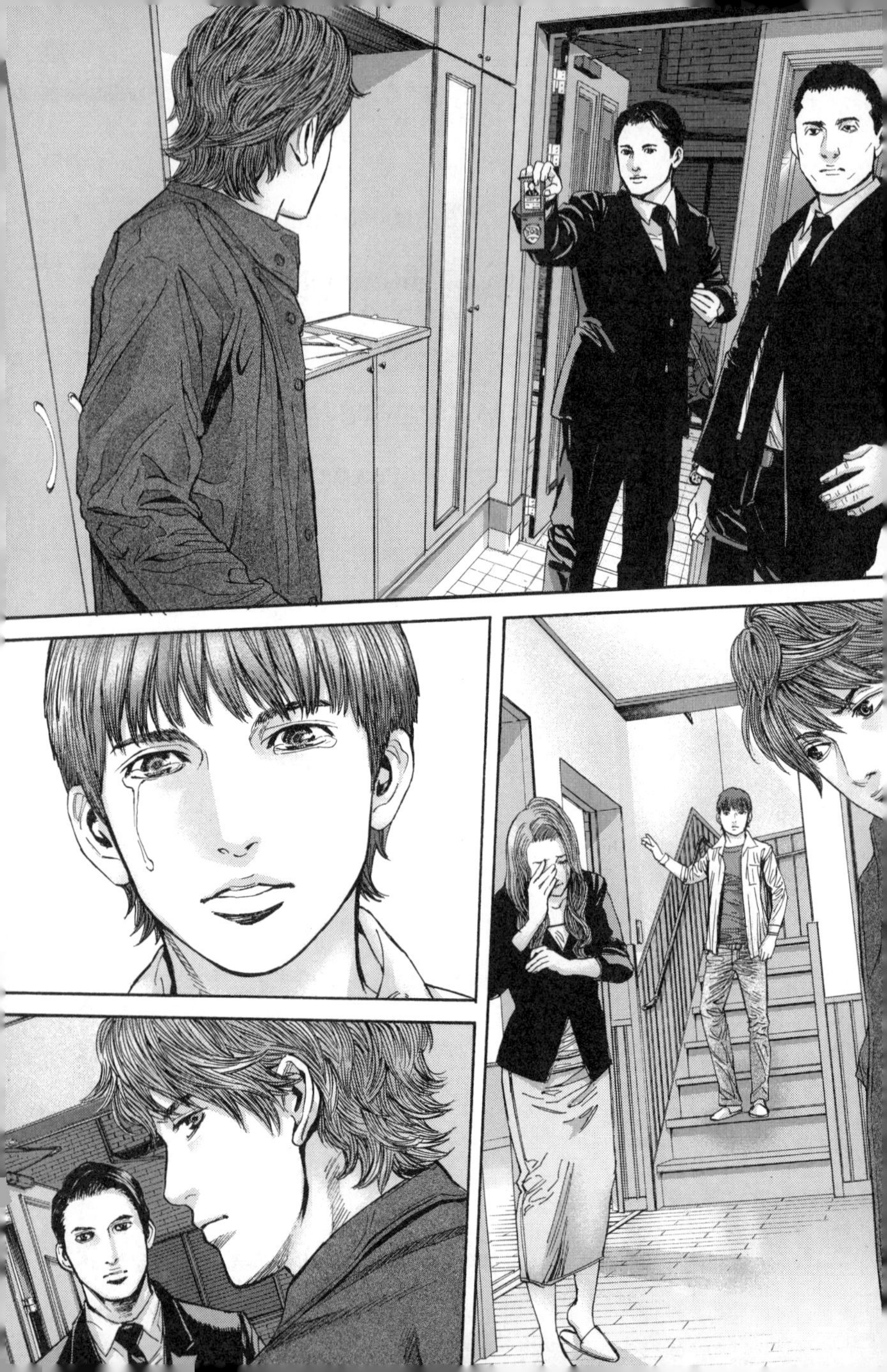

Chapter 9

Juvenile Corrective Institution

Seize the Day!

Juvenile Corrective Institution

Daiki wanted to say goodbye to Seijiro, but the police officers didn't give him the chance. They led him out of the house by the arm and into the waiting patrol car.

Daiki spent several days in a cell at the police station. After some questioning and a brief trial, the authorities decided to send Daiki to a juvenile corrective institution.

WORD LIST			
☐ juvenile corrective institution	(熟)少年鑑別所	☐ spend	(動)過ごす
☐ say goodbye to ~	(熟)~にさよならを言う	☐ cell	(名)独房、監禁室
☐ police officer	(名)警官	☐ police station	(熟)警察署
☐ chance	(名)機会	☐ questioning	(名)尋問
☐ lead	(動)連れて行く	☐ brief	(形)短時間の
☐ out of ~	(熟)~の中から外へ	☐ trial	(名)裁判、公判、審理
☐ waiting	(形)待機している	☐ authority	(名)当局
☐ patrol car	(熟)パトカー	☐ decide to V	(熟)Vすることを決定する
		☐ send	(動)送り出す

Chapter 9

Daiki arrived at the institution in the evening. After some counseling, he was taken to his room. At the institution, six boys shared one room. When Daiki entered the room, the other five boys glared at him. Daiki didn't say anything. He just glared back at them.

It was time for the boys to go to bed and the light went out. When Daiki was lying on his futon, he felt a pillow pushed hard over his face. His arms and legs were pinned down by two boys. He tried to escape

---

WORD LIST

☐ arrive at ~	熟 ～に到着する	☐ go out	熟〈電灯が〉消える
☐ institution	名 少年鑑別所	☐ lie	動 横たわる
☐ counseling	名 カウンセリング、面談	☐ futon	名 布団
☐ take 人 to ~	熟 人を～へ連れて行く	☐ pillow	名 枕
☐ share	動 共有する	☐ over ~	前 ～の上に、～を覆って
☐ enter	動 入る	☐ face	名 顔、顔面
☐ other	形 残り全部の	☐ pin ~ down	熟 ～を押しつけておく
☐ glare at ~	熟 ～をにらみつける	☐ try to V	熟 Vしようと試みる
☐ anything	代〈否定文で〉何も	☐ escape	動 逃げる

Seize the Day! Juvenile Corrective Institution

but couldn't move an inch.

Suddenly, he felt a sharp pain in his belly. Someone was kicking him. The kicks continued. Nobody said a word. The boys took turns kicking Daiki until he gave up trying to escape.

The next morning, when Daiki got up, he had sharp pains all over his body. The other boys were sneering at him. Daiki was feeling angry but he didn't do or say anything then. He could barely stand but did all his daily chores. The night came and the

WORD LIST

☐ not move an inch	熟微動だにしない	☐ get up	熟起き上がる
☐ suddenly	副突然	☐ all over ~	熟~のいたるところで
☐ feel	動感じる、思う	☐ sneer at ~	熟~をあざ笑う
☐ sharp pain	熟鋭い痛み	☐ angry	形怒って
☐ belly	名腹部	☐ anything	代〈否定文で〉何も
☐ continue	動続く	☐ barely	副なんとか、かろうじて
☐ take turns	熟交替でする	☐ daily	形日々の
☐ give up ~	熟~を諦める、止める	☐ chore	名日課
☐ when	接 ..... とき		

light went out again.

This time Daiki was prepared. He was lying with his eyes open.

When he heard the sound of the boys coming toward him, he got up. Now his eyes were accustomed to the dark, and he could see where the boys were.

Daiki kicked the boy in front. He groaned a little. Then he punched him hard in the stomach and knocked him down. The other boys came at him all at once, but they were no match for Daiki. In less

---

WORD LIST

- go out 熟〈電灯が〉消える
- this time 熟今度は
- prepared 形準備ができて
- lie 動横たわる
- eye 名目
- hear 動耳にする
- toward ~ 前~に向かって
- be accustomed to ~ 熟~に慣れている
- dark 名暗がり
- in front 熟正面に
- groan 動うめく
- a little 熟少し、わずか
- punch 動ぶん殴る
- hard 副激しく、強く
- stomach 名腹部、胃
- knock ~ down 熟~をぶちのめす
- all at once 熟一斉に
- be no match for ~ 熟~にはかなわない

than a minute he had beaten them all up.

From the next day, their attitude toward Daiki changed completely. They became quite friendly. For them, having somebody like Daiki in their group was a great advantage over the other groups.

Daiki had several fights with boys from the other groups but he won them all. He was very careful not to be caught by the guards. He didn't attack his opponent's face because if he had left a mark on the guy's face, the guard would have known that they

WORD LIST	
☐ in less than a minute	熟一分足らずで
☐ beat 〜 up	熟〜をぶちのめす
☐ the next day	熟翌日
☐ attitude	名態度
☐ toward 〜	前〜に対して
☐ completely	副完全に
☐ become C	熟Cになる
☐ quite	副かなり
☐ like 〜	前〜のような
☐ advantage	名有利
☐ fight	名戦い、格闘
☐ careful	形注意深い
☐ guard	名看守
☐ opponent	名敵、相手
☐ face	名顔、顔面
☐ leave	動残す
☐ mark	名跡、あざ

had had a fight. Weeks passed like that and Daiki was told that his sentence was finally over. On the morning Daiki left the institution, after finishing breakfast, the guard told all the other boys that Daiki was leaving. The boys stood up one by one and bowed to Daiki. Many boys loved Daiki for his character and his fighting skills.

Suddenly one guard came running into the dining hall and asked Daiki to pack his stuff quickly. He looked very serious. After he finished packing, Daiki

WORD LIST

☐ pass	動〈時が〉過ぎる、経つ	☐ fighting	名戦い、格闘
☐ sentence	名刑、判決	☐ skill	名技術
☐ finally	副ついに、ようやく	☐ come Ving	熟 V しながらやって来る
☐ leave	動去る、離れる	☐ run into ~	熟~に駆け込む
☐ institution	名少年鑑別所	☐ dining hall	熟食堂
☐ finish	動終える	☐ pack	動荷造りする
☐ one by one	熟一人ずつ	☐ stuff	名持ち物
☐ bow	動頭を下げる	☐ look C	熟 C に見える
☐ character	名性格	☐ serious	形真剣な、深刻な

Seize the Day! Juvenile Corrective Institution

was led out and asked to sit in the back seat of a police patrol car. The car started off with the siren going.

"What? What is all this about?" asked Daiki.

The officer in the passenger seat answered, "It's about your brother. He's had an accident."

[To be continued]

WORD LIST

- lead ~ out 熟〜を引っ張り出す
- ask 人 to V 熟人にVするように頼む
- sit 動座る
- back seat 熟後部座席
- police patrol car 熟パトロールカー
- start off 熟出発する
- siren 名サイレン
- ask 動尋ねる
- officer 名警官
- passenger seat 熟助手席
- answer 動答える
- accident 名事故

Chapter 10

A Sudden Farewell

Seize the Day! A Sudden Farewell

A Sudden Farewell

The patrol car arrived at Ofuna and stopped at an intersection. When Daiki got out of the car, he smelled gasoline and rubber. A huge truck had crashed through a guardrail and gasoline was dripping from it. Workers and police officers were running around. Daiki saw his mother sitting on the road, crying. Behind her he could see his brother's bicycle, which was badly mangled.

WORD LIST

- sudden 形突然の
- farewell 名別れ
- patrol car 熟パトカー
- intersection 名交差点
- get out of ~ 熟~から降りる
- smell 動~のにおいがわかる
- gasoline 名ガソリン
- rubber 名ゴム
- huge 形巨大な
- crash through ~ 熟~に大きな音を立ててぶつかる
- guardrail 名ガードレール
- drip 動したたり落ちる
- worker 名作業員
- police officer 名警官
- run around 熟駆け回る
- badly 副ひどく
- mangle 動めちゃくちゃにする

Beside the bicycle he saw Seijiro lying on a stretcher. He was in his school uniform. He seemed to be sleeping. A white cloth was on his head, which seemed a little smaller than usual.

Daiki walked forward and stood in front of his brother. He couldn't believe what he was seeing. It was too surreal. When he squatted down and put his hand on the cloth on Seijiro's head, a police officer grabbed his hand.

"Please don't. I have no right to stop you, but for

WORD LIST			
□ beside ~	前～のそば（隣）に	□ forward	副前へ
□ lie	動横たわる	□ stand	動立つ
□ stretcher	名担架	□ in front of ~	熟～の前に
□ school uniform	熟制服	□ believe	動信じる
□ seem to be C	熟Cのように見える	□ surreal	形超現実的な
□ cloth	名布	□ squat down	熟しゃがむ
□ a little	熟少し、わずか	□ hand	名手
□ than ~	接～よりも、～に比べて	□ grab	動つかむ
□ usual	形いつもの	□ right	名権利

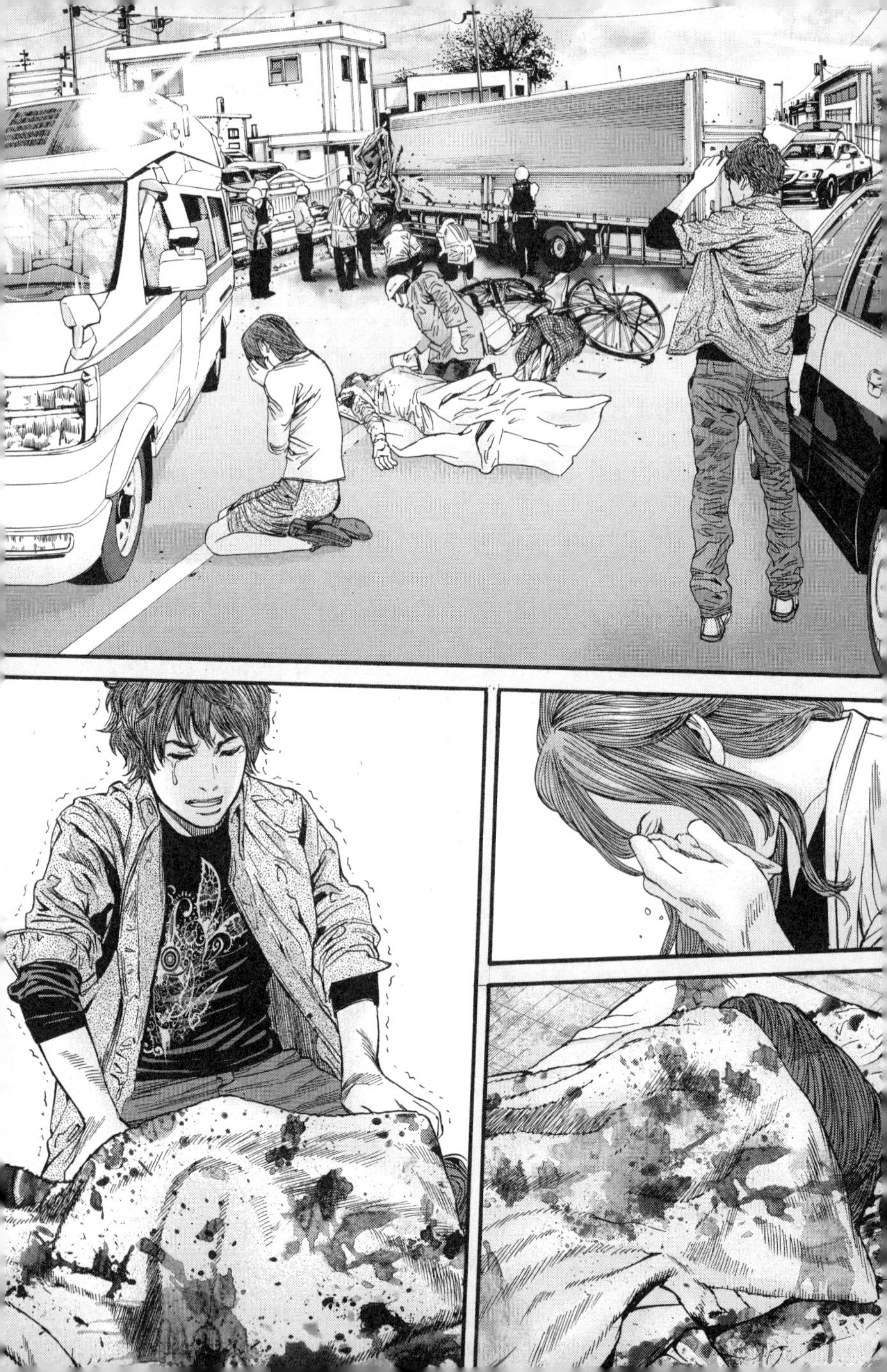

Chapter 10

you and your brother, you shouldn't look. He is not what he was. Please don't look."

Daiki sat on the road, and held his brother's hand. It was cold. Tears rolled down his face.

Seijiro was going to school on his bike when the accident happened. The driver of the truck was looking somewhere else, and didn't stop for the red light. The police explained that Seijiro had lost his life instantly when he was hit.

During the days that followed, Daiki and his

WORD LIST

☐ look	動見る	☐ happen	動起こる
☐ what ~ was	熟昔の~	☐ driver	名運転手
☐ hold	動握る	☐ light	名信号
☐ tear	名涙	☐ explain	動説明する
☐ roll down ~	熟~を流れ落ちる	☐ lose	動失う
☐ face	名顔、顔面	☐ instantly	副直ちに、すぐに
☐ bike	名自転車	☐ hit	動はねる
☐ when	接 ..... とき	☐ during ~	前~の間に
☐ accident	名事故	☐ follow	動続く

Seize the Day! A Sudden Farewell

parents were very busy arranging Seijiro's funeral and answering the reporters from the local media. They didn't have much time to be sad.

Then when it was all over, they were completely exhausted. They had no energy to talk or go anywhere. Daiki spent several days in his room.

Daiki was lying on his bed, staring at the ceiling, when suddenly somebody knocked on the door. It was Jun. He was with Kenji. They were in black overalls. They grabbed Daiki's arms and said, "Let's

WORD LIST

□ be busy Ving	熟 Vするのに忙しい	□ be exhausted	熟 疲れ切った
□ arrange	動 手配する	□ spend	動 過ごす
□ funeral	名 葬儀	□ several	形 いくつかの
□ reporter	名 報道記者	□ lie	動 横たわる
□ local	形 地元の	□ stare at ~	熟 ~をじっと見つめる
□ media	名 報道機関、マスメディア	□ ceiling	名 天井
□ much	形〈否定文で〉大した	□ suddenly	副 突然
□ over	副 終わって	□ overall	名 つなぎ
□ completely	副 完全に	□ grab	動 つかむ

Chapter 10

go."

"Where?" asked Daiki.

"Don't ask. Just get your bike and come with us," they answered.

[To be continued]

WORD LIST

- ask ㊥尋ねる
- just ..... ㊥ただ ..... だけ
- get ㊥乗る
- bike ㊇バイク
- answer ㊥答える

Seize the Day!

Chapter 11

The Last Run

Seize the Day! The Last Run

The Last Run

It was a cold November night. There were no clouds in the sky and the stars were shining brightly. They arrived at the huge parking lot of a theme park. Hundreds of gang members were waiting. They were all wearing black overalls. The engines of their machines were roaring.

The gang leader ordered Daiki to run in front, which was the greatest honor for gang members.

WORD LIST

☐ last	形 最後の	☐ gang member	熟 暴走族のメンバー
☐ run	名 一走り	☐ overall	名 つなぎ
☐ November	名 11月	☐ engine	名 エンジン
☐ shine	動 輝く	☐ roar	動 うなる
☐ brightly	副 明るく	☐ gang leader	熟 暴走族の総長
☐ arrive at 〜	熟 〜に到着する	☐ order 人 to V	熟 人にVするように命じる
☐ huge	形 巨大な	☐ in front	熟 先頭に
☐ parking lot	熟 屋外駐車場	☐ greatest	形 great の最上級
☐ theme park	熟 テーマパーク	☐ honor	名 名誉

Chapter 11

The leader said to Daiki, "We all know about the tragedy that happened to your brother. This is our way of showing respect to you and your brother's soul. After this run, it is up to you whether to quit the gang or stay. Forget everything tonight and run with us to Fuji Speedway."

The motorcycle gangs in the Yokohama area used to gather in a certain place in Yokohama several times a year and head for Mt. Fuji. Their goal was the parking lot of the racing circuit named Fuji Speedway.

WORD LIST

- tragedy 名悲劇
- show 動証明する
- respect 名尊敬
- soul 名魂
- be up to ～ 熟～次第で
- whether ..... 接 .....(する)かどうか
- quit 動辞める
- gang 名暴走族
- forget 動忘れる
- motorcycle gang 熟暴走族
- used to V 熟よくVしたものだ
- gather 動集まる
- certain 形ある
- head for ～ 熟～に向かってまっすぐ進む
- racing circuit 熟レース場
- name 動名前を付ける

Seize the Day! The Last Run

Especially on New Year's Eve, many gangs from Yokohama and neighboring areas used to join together, and thousands of gang members would head for Mt. Fuji. They almost never reached their destination because of police interference. They usually were caught by the police or sent back. Still, it was their dream to reach Fuji Speedway.

It was almost two in the morning. The gangs started with Daiki in front. Strangely there was no police interference that night. Before they left the

WORD LIST

- especially　副特に
- New Year's Eve 熟大晦日
- neighboring　形近所の
- used to V　熟よく V したものだ
- join　動加わる
- thousands of 〜 熟何千という〜
- head for 〜　熟〜に向かってまっすぐ進む
- almost　副ほとんど
- reach　動到着する
- destination　名目的地
- because of 〜 熟〜のために、〜のせいで
- interference　名妨害
- usually　副いつも
- in front　熟先頭に
- strangely　副不思議なことに
- leave　動去る、離れる

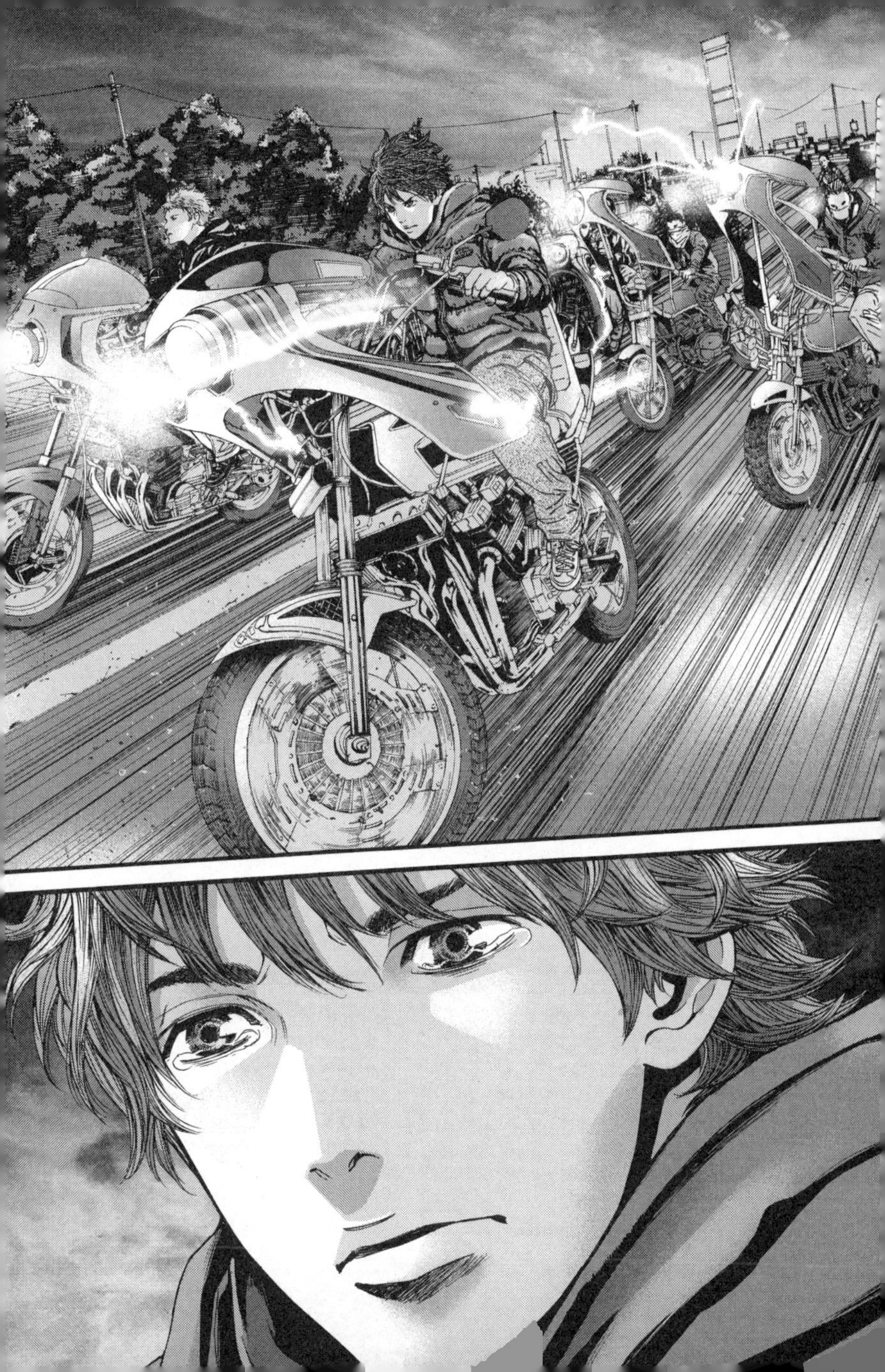

Seize the Day! The Last Run

Yokohama area, other groups joined them. Now there were over one thousand people. When they entered Shizuoka prefecture, several police patrol cars appeared from behind. The voice from the loudspeaker said to the gang, "Stop now. Stop immediately, or we'll arrest you."

The gang that was running at the end of the line slowed down and stopped in front of the patrol cars in order to let the others go. Many more police cars came, but again other gangs sacrificed themselves in

WORD LIST

- when ..... 接 ..... とき
- enter 動入る
- prefecture 名県
- police patrol car 熟パトロールカー
- appear 動現れる
- loudspeaker 名拡声器
- immediately 動ただちに
- arrest 動逮捕する
- at the end of ～ 熟～の最後部に
- slow down 熟速度を遅くする
- in front of ～ 熟～の前に
- patrol car 熟パトカー
- in order to V 熟Vするために
- let O V 熟OにVさせてやる
- the others 熟他の人たち
- more 形より多くの
- police car 熟パトカー
- sacrifice 動犠牲にする

Chapter 11

order to let Daiki's gang go on.

Finally Daiki and others entered the parking lot of Fuji Speedway. It was the first time that Daiki's gang had reached the goal.

Now it was six o'clock. Daiki, Jun and Kenji were watching a beautiful sunrise, sitting on their bikes and talking. That morning they decided to quit the gang and become adults.

[To be continued]

WORD LIST

□ gang	名暴走族	□ sunrise	名日の出
□ go on	熟進み続ける	□ sit	動座る
□ finally	副ついに、ようやく	□ bike	名バイク
□ others	代他の人たち	□ talk	動話す
□ parking lot	熟屋外駐車場	□ decide to V	熟Vすることを決心する
□ the first time	熟初めて	□ quit	動辞める
□ reach	動到着する	□ become C	熟Cになる
□ o'clock	副時	□ adult	名大人
□ goal	名目標、目的		

Seize the Day!

Chapter 12

Daiki and Yumi

Seize the Day! Daiki and Yumi

Daiki and Yumi

Daiki, Jun and Kenji got back to their normal life as high school students. Teachers said that if they kept attending classes, they would have no problem graduating, so they came to school every day, even though they slept and read comic books in classes like everybody else.

On the day of the high school graduation ceremony, when Daiki was going home from the

---

WORD LIST

- get back to ～ 熟～に戻る
- normal life 熟普通の生活
- as ～ 前～として
- high school 熟高校
- if ..... 接もし..... ならば
- keep Ving 熟Vし続ける
- attend 動出席する
- have no problem Ving
  熟Vすることに全く問題はない
- graduate 動卒業する
- so 接だから
- every day 熟毎日
- even though ..... 熟..... であるけれども
- comic book 熟マンガ本
- like ～ 前～のように
- else 副その他に
- on the day of ～ 熟～の日に
- graduation ceremony 熟卒業式

Chapter 12

station, he saw a girl surrounded by some delinquent boys. From the uniform she was wearing, Daiki knew she was a student at Yamashita High, one of the most prestigious high schools in Yokohama. Her hair was black and straight. She had beautiful eyes, but they were full of tears.

Daiki walked up to the girl, glared at the boys and said, "My name is Daiki Okuda from Seikai High. Nice to meet you all, guys. Do you guys want to have some fun?"

WORD LIST

□ station	名駅	□ straight	形まっすぐな
□ surround	動囲む	□ eye	名目
□ some	形いくらかの	□ be full of ～	熟～でいっぱいである
□ delinquent	形非行の	□ tear	名涙
□ uniform	名制服	□ walk up to ～	熟～に近寄る
□ wear	動着ている	□ glare at ～	熟～をにらみつける
□ know	動わかる	□ Nice to meet you.	熟初めまして
□ prestigious	形一流の、有名な	□ guy	名〈呼びかけで〉君
□ hair	名髪の毛	□ want to V	熟 V したいと思う

Seize the Day! Daiki and Yumi

Hearing the name, Daiki Okuda, the boys turned pale. Some of them were trembling with fear. One of them said, "Well, we were just showing her the way to the station. Nice to meet you, too. I've heard a lot about you. Excuse us. We'll leave now. Bye."

After the boys left, the girl said to Daiki, "Thank you for saving me. My name is Yumi. Yumi Yamamoto. Your name's Daiki, isn't it?" She said, looking straight into his eyes.

Daiki had gone out with many girls, but this was

WORD LIST

☐ hear	動耳にする	☐ way to ~	熟～への道
☐ turn	動～になる	☐ a lot	熟よく、とても
☐ pale	形青ざめた	☐ Excuse us.	熟失礼します
☐ some	代～する人もいる	☐ leave	動去る、離れる
☐ tremble with ~	熟～で震える	☐ after	接～の後に（で）
☐ fear	名恐れ	☐ thank you for Ving	
☐ well	間ええと		熟 V してくれてありがとう
☐ just	副ただ.....だけ	☐ save	動救う
☐ show	動教える	☐ look into ~	熟～の中をのぞく

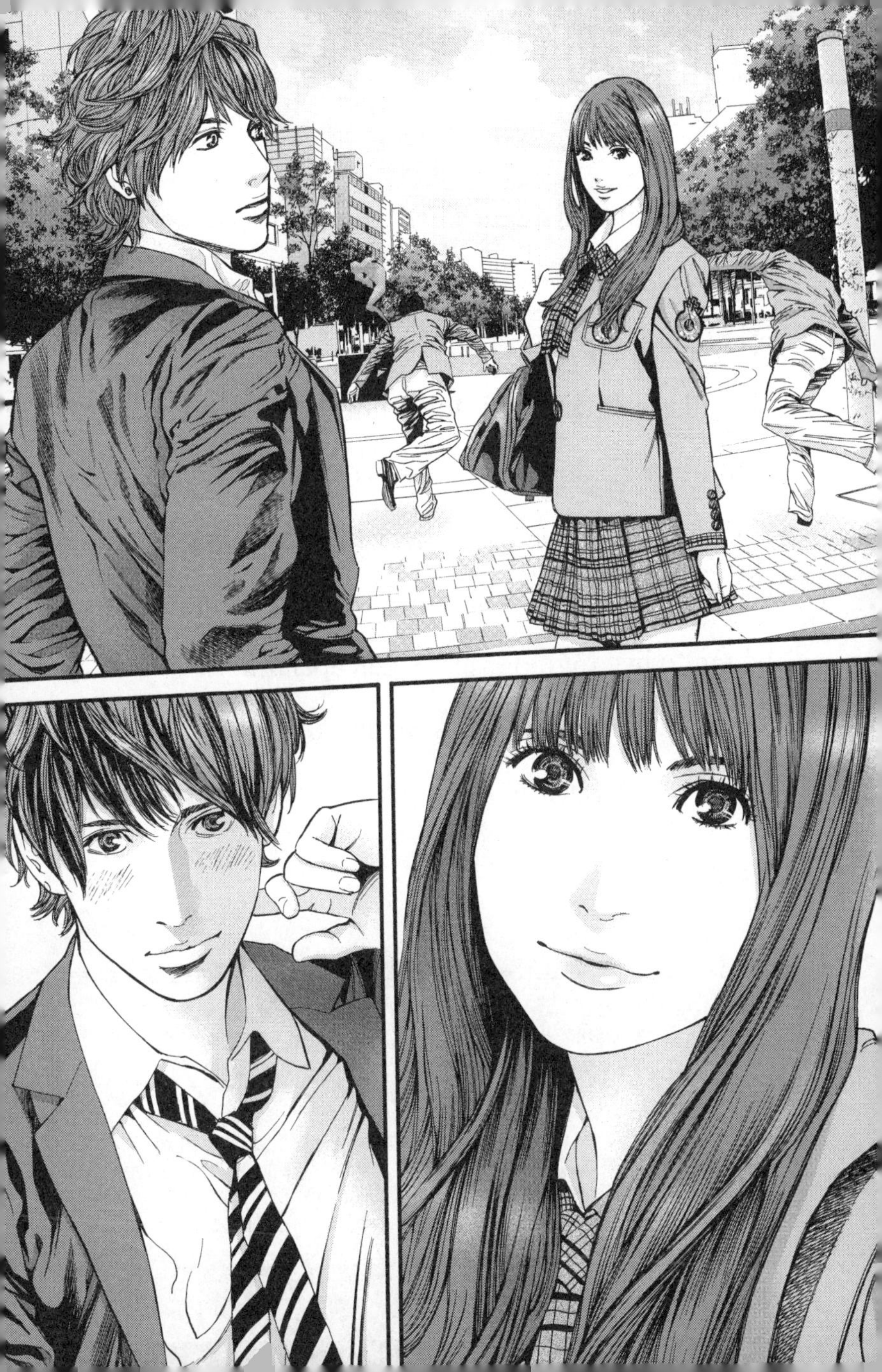

Seize the Day! Daiki and Yumi

the first time his heart had pounded this hard. He was blushing. Looking at him, Yumi smiled and said, "Buy me a cup of coffee, shy boy."

This is how Daiki and Yumi started going out. After they graduated from high school, Daiki became a used car salesman and Yumi entered a college. She also worked as a part-time fashion model. They began to live together in a small apartment.

Jun began to work at a pachinko parlor, and Kenji became a yakuza like his brother. They each went

---

WORD LIST

- the first time 熟初めて
- pound 動〈心臓が〉どきどきする
- blush 動顔を赤らめる
- look at ~ 熟~を見る
- a cup of ~ 熟一杯の~
- This is how ~ 熟こういう風に~した
- start Ving 熟Vし始める
- go out ~ 熟~と付き合う
- graduate from ~ 熟~を卒業する
- become C 熟Cになる
- used car 熟中古車
- salesman 名男性販売員
- enter 動入学する
- also 副~もまた、さらに
- part-time 熟アルバイトの
- fashion model 熟ファッションモデル
- begin to V 熟Vし始める
- live 動暮らす

Chapter 12

their own way and saw less and less of each other.

In the first few months after he started to work, Daiki earned only eighty thousand yen a month, while Yumi earned twice that amount from her part-time job. Daiki loved Yumi very much, and he believed Yumi loved him the same way. He worked very hard to be a person worthy of her. Daiki worked every day until late at night. He usually came home after ten looking forward to having the meal Yumi had prepared for him with a glass of beer.

WORD LIST

- pachinko parlor 熟 パチンコ屋
- like ~ 前 ~と同じように
- own 形 自分自身の
- less and less 熟 ますます少なく
- each other 熟 お互い
- earn 動 稼ぐ
- while ..... 接 だが一方 .....
- twice 副 2倍
- amount 名 総額
- very much 熟 非常に、とても
- worthy of ~ 熟 ~にふさわしい
- usually 副 いつも
- after ~ 前 ~過ぎに
- look forward to Ving 熟 Vするのを楽しみに待つ
- meal 名 食事
- prepare for ~ 熟 ~に備える、準備する
- a glass of ~ 熟 グラス一杯の~

Seize the Day! Daiki and Yumi

One day when he got back to their apartment, Yumi was not there, and all her stuff was gone. Daiki found a note on the table.

[To be continued]

WORD LIST

- one day　　　熟ある日
- when .....　　接 ..... とき
- get back to ～　熟～に戻る
- apartment　　名アパート
- stuff　　　　名持ち物
- gone　　　　形なくなった
- find　　　　動見つける
- note　　　　名メモ
- table　　　　名テーブル、食卓

Seize the Day!

Chapter 13

He's Different from You.

He's Different from You.

The note said, "Daiki, I know you are a very nice person, but I can't see any future with you. I'm sorry. Please don't look for me.

Good Bye. Yumi."

He remembered what Yumi had said the day before. "I'm worried. I'm worried about our future. This is so different from the life I had been dreaming of. I don't know whether I love you any more." She

WORD LIST

- be different from ～ 熟 ～とは違った
- note 名 メモ
- know 動 知る、わかる
- person 名 人間
- any 形〈否定文で〉何も
- future 名 将来
- sorry 形 すまなく思って
- look for ～ 熟 ～を捜す
- remember 動 思い出す
- the day before 熟 前日
- worried 形 心配な
- so 副 とても、非常に
- life 名 生活
- dream of ～ 熟 ～を夢見る
- whether..... 接 .....（する）かどうか
- love 動 愛する
- any more 熟 これ以上

was crying when she had said that.

Daiki thought that she had left him because of money. He thought, to get her back, he had to earn much more. He decided to look her up after he had become the top salesperson in his company.

He thought just working hard was not enough. He bought books about sales techniques and studied them. Also, he observed the way the other salespeople sold cars. He noticed that instead of finding new connections, utilizing the connections he

WORD LIST

- leave 動去る、離れる
- because of ~ 熟~のために、~のせいで
- get ~ back 熟~を取り戻す
- earn 動稼ぐ
- much more 熟もっとたくさん
- decide to V 熟 V することを決心する
- look ~ up 熟~を訪ねる
- become C 熟 C になる
- salesperson 名販売員
- enough 形十分な
- technique 名技術、コツ
- also 接その上、さらに
- observe 動観察する
- salespeople 名販売員
- notice 動気付く
- instead of ~ 熟~ではなくて
- utilize 動利用する、役立たせる
- connection 名関係、つながり

Seize the Day! He's Different from You.

already had was very important to sell cars.

Daiki called all the former members of his motorcycle gang. Quite a lot of them had just gotten their car licenses and were about to buy cars.

They gladly bought cars from Daiki. Some of them sold their old cars to be able to buy new ones from Daiki.

In just two months Daiki became the top salesperson in the company. His monthly salary skyrocketed. He even got a special bonus from the

---

WORD LIST

□ call	動電話をかける	□ month	名(暦の) 月
□ all the ~	熟すべての~	□ become C	熟 C になる
□ former	形昔の、前の	□ salesperson	名販売員
□ motorcycle gang	熟暴走族	□ company	名会社
□ quite a lot of ~	熟かなり多くの~	□ monthly salary	熟月給
□ license	名免許証	□ skyrocket	動急上昇する
□ be about to V	熟まさにVしようとしている	□ even	副~までも
□ gladly	副喜んで	□ special	形特別な
□ be able to V	熟 Vすることができる	□ bonus	名賞与

Chapter 13

company owner, Mr. Hirasawa.

Daiki decided to look Yumi up and call her. After asking a lot of friends, he finally learned Yumi's number and called her.

"Hey, Yumi. Sorry to have worried you so much. I understand your feelings about our future, but the problems are solved now. I became the top salesman in the company, and Mr. Hirasawa promised to pay me three hundred fifty thousand yen starting next month. I even got a special bonus of five hundred

WORD LIST			
□ owner	名所有者、持ち主	□ worry	動心配させる
□ decide to V	熟Vすることを決心する	□ so	副とても、非常に
□ look ~ up	熟~を訪ねる	□ feeling	名感情、気持ち
□ after ~	前~の後に(で)	□ problem	名問題
□ finally	副ついに、ようやく	□ solve	動解決する
□ learn	動知る	□ salesman	名男性販売員
□ number	名電話番号	□ promise to V	熟Vすると約束する
□ sorry to V		□ pay	動支払う
熟Vしたことをすまなく思って		□ yen	名円

Seize the Day! He's Different from You.

thousand yen. Let's celebrate. What do you want to do and what do you want to eat? Name anything," said Daiki.

"No, Daiki. You don't understand. It's not about that. It's about something else. Well ... To tell the truth, I met somebody else. He's also a part-time model, and I'm going out with him," answered Yumi.

"What? You're going out with somebody else? What? What's so special about him? Am I not enough for you? Why, Yumi?"

WORD LIST

- yen 名円
- celebrate 動祝う
- want to V 熟 V したいと思う
- name 動決める
- anything 代何でも
- something else 熟何か他のもの
- well 間ええと、そうね
- to tell the truth 熟実を言えば
- meet 動出会う
- somebody else 熟他の誰か
- also 副〜もまた、さらに
- part-time 熟アルバイトの
- model 名モデル
- go out with 〜 熟〜と付き合う
- answer 動答える
- so 副とても、非常に
- special 形特別な
- enough 形十分な

"Well. He's not like you. He's very smart. He studies law in college. He goes to Seito University. He says he's going to be a lawyer. Anyway ... I'm sorry, but please don't call me any more." She hung up the phone.

[To be continued]

WORD LIST

□ like ~	前～のような
□ smart	形賢い、利口な
□ law	名法律
□ college	名大学
□ university	名大学
□ lawyer	名弁護士
□ anyway	副ともかく
□ sorry	形すまなく思って
□ call	動電話をかける
□ any more	熟これ以上
□ hang up ~	熟～を切る
□ phone	名電話

Seize the Day!

Chapter 14

I'll Show Them.

Seize the Day! I'll Show Them.

I'll Show Them.

Yumi's words made Daiki feel completely worthless. He remembered Makoto's expression on the day of the announcement and how he had been treated by his teachers at junior high school. Then something sparked in his mind.

He decided to do it again. He decided to study for the examination.

It was not that he wanted to go to college. It was

WORD LIST

- word ㊂言葉
- make O V ㊥OにVさせる
- feel ㊙感じる、思う
- completely ㊨完全に
- worthless ㊢価値のない
- remember ㊙思い出す
- expression ㊂表情
- on the day of ～ ㊥～の日に
- announcement ㊂発表、公表
- how ㊨どのようにして
- treat ㊙扱う
- junior high school ㊥中学校
- something ㊝何か
- spark ㊙火花を散らす、輝く
- decide to V ㊥Vすることを決心する
- examination ㊂試験
- want to V ㊥Vしたいと思う
- college ㊂大学

Chapter 14

his way of fighting against the unfairness of society. He thought that if school records and prestigious jobs were so important, he would achieve them, achieve them all. The next morning he handed in his resignation to Mr. Hirasawa.

When he heard the reason, Mr. Hirasawa didn't try to stop Daiki. Instead he cheered him on.

Daiki was twenty years old then and it was already December.

There was only a little over two months before the

WORD LIST

□ fighting	名戦い、格闘	□ resignation	名辞表
□ against ~	前〜に反して	□ when	接 ..... とき
□ unfairness	名不公平さ	□ hear	動耳にする
□ society	名社会	□ reason	名理由
□ record	名成績	□ try to V	熟 V しようと試みる
□ prestigious	形一流の、有名な	□ instead	副それどころか
□ so	副とても、非常に	□ cheer ~ on	熟〜を励ます
□ achieve	動獲得する	□ a little	熟少し、わずか
□ hand in ~	熟〜を手渡す	□ over ~	前〜以上

Seize the Day! I'll Show Them.

exam. He chose English, Japanese and Japanese history as the subjects for the entrance examination.

Daiki's strategy was to reactivate the knowledge he had had before the entrance examination for junior high school. In Japan the entrance exams for prestigious junior high schools are very difficult. Parts of them are as difficult as college entrance exams. Daiki started by recalling what he had learned at juku when he was in elementary school. After one month, he was doing pretty well in Japanese

---

WORD LIST

- choose 動選ぶ
- Japanese 名国語
- Japanese history 熟日本史
- as ~ 前~として
- subject 名科目、教科
- entrance examination 熟入学試験
- strategy 名戦略
- reactivate 動復活させる
- knowledge 名知識
- junior high school 熟中学校
- entrance exam 熟入学試験
- prestigious 形一流の、有名な
- part 名一部分
- as A as B 熟Bと同じほどA
- recall 動思い出す
- when ..... 接.....とき
- elementary school 熟小学校
- pretty well 熟かなりよく

and Japanese history. His scores on the practice exams for these two subjects were over the required levels.

However, he didn't know what to do about English. He didn't know how to read even simple words like "you" and "them" because he had quit studying when he entered junior high, when English classes started. He decided to concentrate on the other two subjects to cover the low score he would get in English. To do that, it meant he had to get over 90 percent in these

WORD LIST

□ score	名点数、成績	□ quit Ving	熟 V するのを止める
□ practice exam	熟模擬試験	□ enter	動入学する
□ over ~	前~を超えて	□ junior high	熟中学校
□ required	形必須の	□ decide to V	熟 V することを決心する
□ however	副しかしながら	□ concentrate on ~	熟~に集中する
□ how to V	熟 V する方法	□ cover	動補う
□ even	副~（で）さえ	□ mean	動意味する
□ word	名単語	□ have to V	熟 V しなければならない
□ like ~	前~のような	□ over ~	前~以上

Seize the Day! I'll Show Them.

two subjects. He had no time to waste.

It was the middle of January. Daiki had just one month until the first entrance examination. On the day before Coming-of-Age Day, he got a call from Jun.

In Japan, municipal governments hold coming-of-age ceremonies for people who turn twenty in that school year. Jun said that after the ceremony a lot of old friends would have a huge party and asked Daiki to join.

WORD LIST

- subject 名科目、教科
- waste 動無駄にする
- the middle of ～ 熟～の中頃
- January 名1月
- until ～ 前～までずっと
- entrance examination 熟入学試験
- on the day before ～ 熟～の前日に
- Coming-of-Age Day 熟成人の日
- get a call 熟電話を取る
- municipal government 熟市政
- hold 動行なう
- coming-of-age ceremony 熟成人式
- turn 動～になる
- ceremony 名式
- a lot of ～ 熟たくさんの～
- huge 形巨大な
- ask 人 to V 熟人にVするように頼む
- join 動加わる

Chapter 14

Daiki had planned to attend the ceremony, but he intended to come home immediately afterwards and study. He didn't want to waste any time. At the same time, he really wanted to see his old friends.

Part of him thought that it would be okay to party for just one night to relieve his stress.

Suddenly Daiki stood up from his desk, with a knife in his hand and began to cut the suit that his mother had prepared for him for the ceremony. Now he wouldn't be able to attend the ceremony itself

WORD LIST

- plan to V 熟 Vするつもりである
- attend 動 出席する
- intend to V 熟 Vするつもりである
- immediately 副 ただちに
- afterwards 副 その後、後で
- any 形〈否定文で〉少しも
- at the same time 熟 同時に
- really 副 本当に
- part 名 一部分
- relieve 動 解消する
- stress 名 ストレス
- suddenly 副 突然
- stand up 熟 立ち上がる
- knife 名 ナイフ、包丁
- begin to V 熟 Vし始める
- suit 名 スーツ
- prepare for ～ 熟 ～に備える、準備する
- be able to V 熟 Vすることができる

Seize the Day! I'll Show Them.

because he had ruined the only suit he had. He was in tears.

[To be continued]

WORD LIST

- because ..... 接 ..... なので
- ruin 動めちゃくちゃにする
- the only ~ 熟たった一つの~
- suit 名スーツ
- be in tears 熟涙を浮かべて

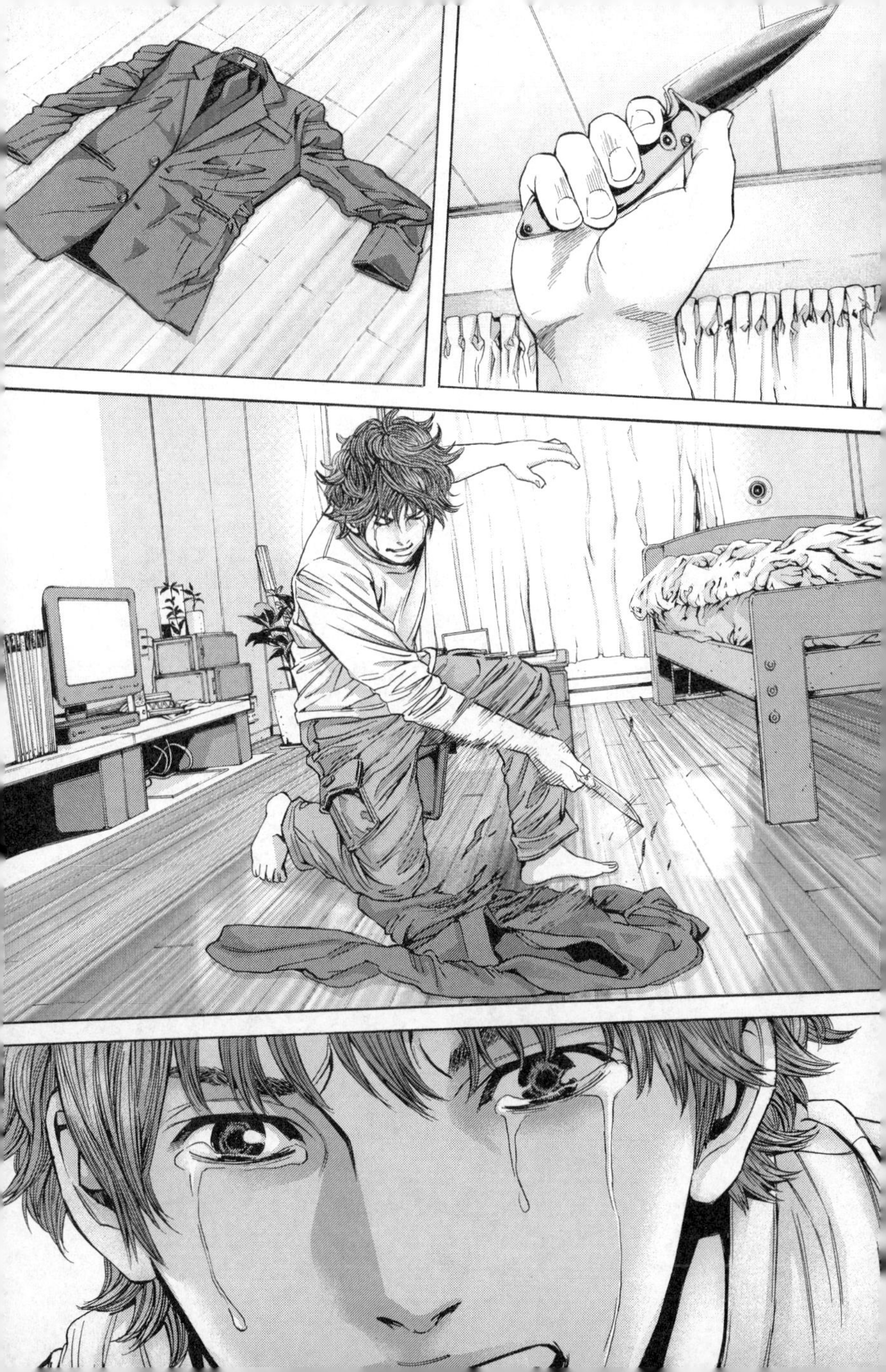

Seize the Day!

Chapter 15

Is This My Mission in Life?

Seize the Day! Is This My Mission in Life?

Is This My Mission in Life?

Daiki didn't rest even for a single day. He only slept three to five hours a night. Days passed like that until the day of the first examination finally came. The first exam was for Gakkoku University, Daiki's first choice. Gakkoku University was famous for its Japanese literature studies, and Daiki wanted to study Japanese classics there.

The first subject was English. He did all he could,

WORD LIST

mission	名使命	finally	副ついに、ようやく
rest	動休む	exam	名試験
even	副〜（で）さえ	first choice	熟第一志望
single	形ただ一つの	be famous for 〜	熟〜で有名である
night	名夜	Japanese literature	熟日本文学
pass	動〈時が〉過ぎる、経つ	want to V	熟 V したいと思う
like 〜	前〜のように	Japanese classics	熟日本の古典
until 〜	前〜までずっと	subject	名科目、教科
examination	名試験	English	名英語

Chapter 15

but he knew he got most of the questions wrong. He didn't care. It was as he had expected.

The second subject was Japanese. Daiki thought he had gotten over 90 percent of the questions right. The third subject was Japanese history. When the test started, Daiki wanted to scream with joy. Most of the questions were quite similar to what he had studied the week before. He was almost certain that he would pass the exam. His guess was right. He passed the exam of Gakkoku University. Not only

---

WORD LIST

- most of ~ 熟〜のほとんど
- care 動気にする
- as ..... 接 ..... のように
- expect 動予想する
- Japanese 名国語
- over ~ 前〜以上
- Japanese history 熟日本史
- scream 動叫ぶ
- with joy 熟喜んで
- quite 副かなり
- be similar to ~ 熟〜とよく似た
- before 副以前に
- almost 副ほとんど
- be certain that S V 熟 S が V するのを確信している
- pass 動合格する、受かる
- guess 名推測

Seize the Day! Is This My Mission in Life?

that, he passed all the other examinations he took, too.

After entering Gakkoku University, Daiki began to study Japanese literature and to teach Japanese and Japanese history in a juku, too. His lessons were very popular among students. Soon he was the top teacher at the juku. Daiki loved teaching and he loved his students. He now knew the power of teaching. He was surprised how his words could motivate students and change their lives. He was

WORD LIST

☐ pass	動合格する、受かる	☐ Japanese history	熟日本史
☐ all the ～	熟すべての～	☐ popular	形人気のある、評判の良い
☐ examination	名試験	☐ among ～	前～の間で
☐ take	動〈試験を〉受ける	☐ soon	副すぐに
☐ after ～	前～の後に（で）	☐ power	名力
☐ enter	動入学する	☐ be surprised	熟驚く
☐ begin to V	熟 V し始める	☐ how	副 ...... するということ
☐ Japanese literature	熟日本文学	☐ word	名言葉
☐ Japanese	名国語	☐ motivate	動意欲を与える

now convinced that through this job he could save many boys and girls who were struggling like he had been.

Impressed by his teaching skills, the owner of the juku advised Daiki to become a prep school teacher after graduation, so Daiki decided to take the examination for Tokushin Seminar.

Tokushin Seminar is the biggest prep school in Japan, and its teachers are considered the best of the best in the education industry. Only one teacher in

---

WORD LIST

- be convinced 熟確信している
- through ～ 前～を通じて
- save 動救う
- struggle 動奮闘する、努力する
- like ～ 前～のように
- be impressed by ～ 熟～に感心する
- teaching skill 熟技術指導
- owner 名所有者、持ち主
- advise 人 to V 熟人にVするように勧める
- become C 熟Cになる
- prep school 熟予備校
- graduation 名卒業
- so 接だから
- decide to V 熟Vすることを決心する
- biggest 形 big の最上級
- be considered C 熟Cとみなされている
- the best of the best 熟一流中の一流
- education industry 熟教育業界

Seize the Day! Is This My Mission in Life?

several hundred passes its employment exam.

Daiki passed the exam. Not only did he pass the exam, but he also got the highest score in the history of Tokushin Seminar.

[To be continued]

WORD LIST

- several 形いくつかの
- hundred 名100人
- pass 動合格する、受かる
- employment exam 熟入社試験
- not only A, but also B 熟Aばかりでなくbも
- get 動得る
- highest 形highの最上級
- score 名点数、成績
- history 名過去、史上

Chapter 16

Stairs

Seize the Day!

Stairs

On the day Daiki got the results that he had passed the examination, he had dinner with Mr. Hirasawa in Yokohama. Mr. Hirasawa was very glad to see Daiki after such a long time. They had dinner together and talked for a long time.

Mr. Hirasawa offered Daiki a ride and they headed for Ofuna together, with Daiki in the passenger seat.

It was all so sudden. Daiki didn't know what had

Chapter 16

happened. He felt like his body was floating. When he looked back, he could see Mr. Hirasawa and himself. Both of them were covered in blood. He thought he was dreaming, but the dream was very real.

In front of him, he saw stairs leading up. Daiki started to climb up the stairs slowly. When he had almost got to the top, he couldn't believe what he was seeing.

He saw his brother, Seijiro, there. Seijiro was

WORD LIST

- happen — 動起こる
- feel like ..... — 熟 ..... のような気がする
- float — 動浮かぶ
- when ..... — 接 ..... とき
- look back — 熟振り返る
- both — 代両者とも
- be covered in blood — 熟血まみれである
- real — 形現実の
- in front of ~ — 熟~の前に
- lead up — 熟通じる
- start to V — 熟V し始める
- climb up the stairs — 熟階段を上る
- slowly — 副ゆっくりと
- almost — 副ほとんど
- get to ~ — 熟~に到着する
- believe — 動信じる

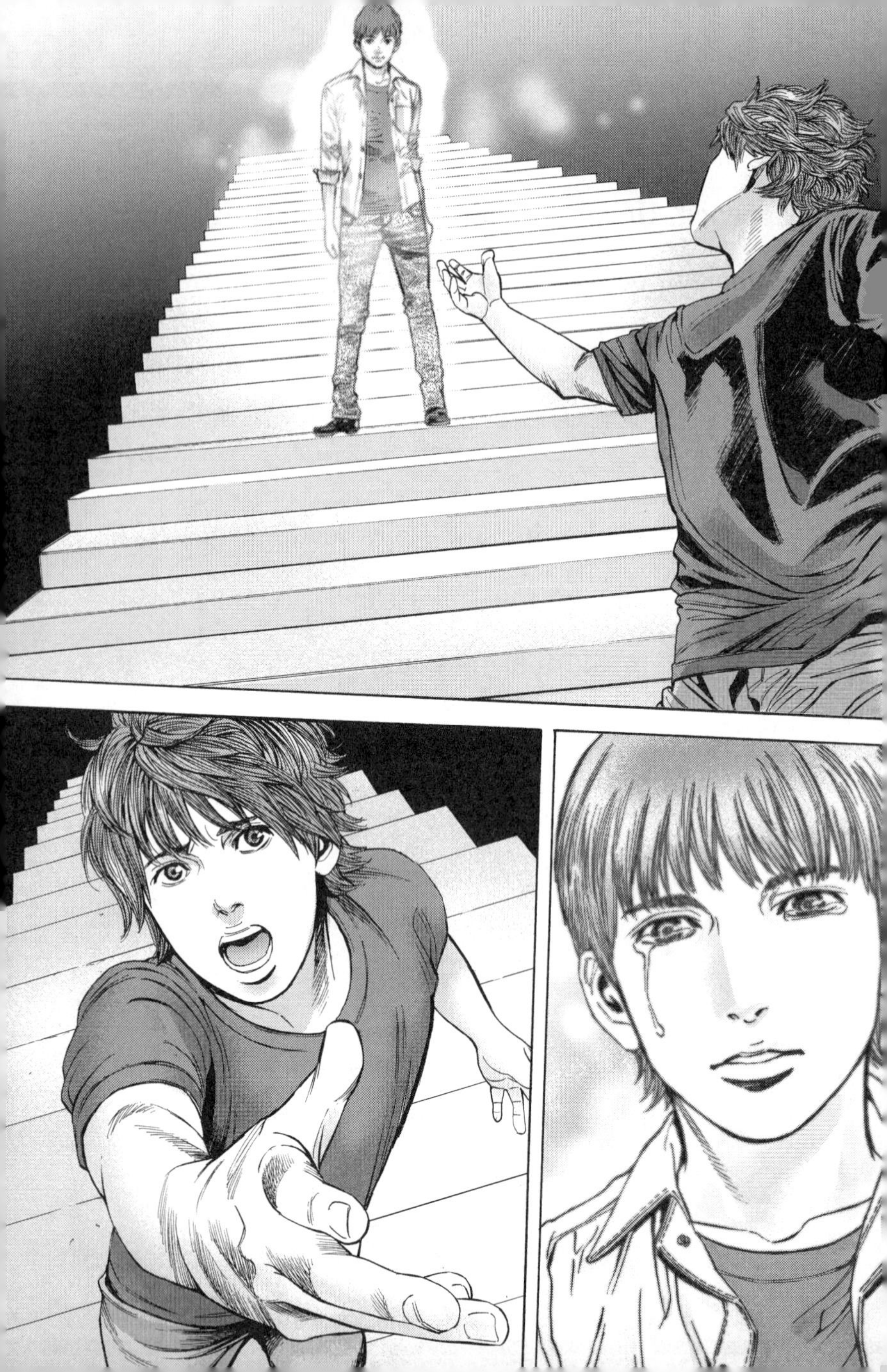

smiling at Daiki, his eyes full of tears. They stood looking at each other for a while. Tears rolled down Daiki's cheeks.

Daiki reached his hands out to touch his brother, but when Daiki's hands were about to touch Seijiro's body, suddenly Seijiro pushed Daiki very hard. Daiki tumbled all the way back down the stairs.

Daiki woke up on a bed in a hospital. He learned that Mr. Hirasawa had fallen asleep while driving and his car, crashed through a guardrail and rolled over.

WORD LIST

□ smile at ~	熟 ~に微笑みかける	□ all the way	熟 ずっと
□ be full of ~	熟 ~でいっぱいである	□ stairs	名 階段
□ for a while	熟 しばらく	□ learn	動 知る
□ roll down ~	熟 ~を流れ落ちる	□ fall asleep	熟 寝入る
□ cheek	名 頬	□ while	接 ..... している間に
□ reach ~ out	熟 ~を伸ばす	□ crash through ~	熟 ~に大きな音を立ててぶつかる
□ touch	動 触れる	□ guardrail	名 ガードレール
□ be about to V	熟 まさにVしようとしている	□ roll over	熟 転がる、反転する
□ tumble	動 転落する		

Seize the Day! Stairs

Both of them had been in a coma for two days.

After he left the hospital, Daiki began to teach at Tokushin Seminar. He enjoyed teaching and was thankful for everyone he had met in his life, especially his brother.

Daiki now knew what his brother had wanted to say there at the top of the stairs. He knew Seijiro wanted Daiki to live, to live and enjoy a wonderful life.

[To be continued]

WORD LIST

□ both	代両者とも	□ want to V	熟Vしたいと思う
□ coma	名昏睡状態	□ the top of ～	熟～のてっぺん
□ after	接～の後に（で）	□ live	動生きる
□ leave	動去る、離れる	□ want 人 to V	熟人にVして欲しいと思う
□ begin to V	熟Vし始める	□ life	名人生
□ enjoy Ving	熟Vすることを楽しむ		
□ thankful	形感謝している		
□ everyone	代すべての人		
□ especially	副特に		

Seize the Day!

Chapter 17

Believe in Yourself, Okay?

Believe in Yourself, Okay?

Daiki Okuda has taught for over twenty five years now. He always says to his students, "A lot of things can happen in your life. Sometimes things might not go well and you might make mistakes, big mistakes like I did, but remember that you can always change. Life is wonderful. Be thankful that you're alive. Don't waste even a moment of your life. I know this society is unfair. Well, life is unfair, but you can overcome it if

WORD LIST

believe in 〜	熟〜の価値を信じる	remember	動覚えている
over 〜	前〜以上	thankful	形感謝している
a lot of 〜	熟たくさんの〜	alive	形生きている
happen	動起こる	waste	動無駄にする
sometimes	副時々	even	副〜(で)さえ
might V	熟Vするかもしれない	moment	名瞬間、一瞬
go well	熟うまくいく	society	名社会
mistake	名間違い	unfair	形不公平な
like 〜	前〜のように	well	間まあ

you put in the effort. So guys, listen carefully. You're never fools, even if sometimes you think you are. If you don't give up, you can achieve anything. Believe in yourself, okay?"

The End

WORD LIST

☐ overcome	動克服する、打ち勝つ
☐ if	接もし ..... ならば
☐ put in ~	熟～をつぎ込む
☐ effort	名努力
☐ so	接だから
☐ guy	名〈呼びかけで〉君
☐ carefully	副注意深く、気を付けて
☐ never	副決して～ない
☐ fool	名ばか者
☐ even if	熟たとえ ..... でも
☐ think	動思う
☐ give up ~	熟～を諦める、止める
☐ achieve	動成し遂げる、達成する
☐ anything	代何でも

東進が開発したWEBブラウザ版「教育ゲーム」

Online Edutainment
みんなの一問一答オンライン
by Toshin Books

― Study Monster ―

基本無料※

みんなとつながる、みんなで学ぶ。

▼ゲームの目標・目的
- 大学受験
- 英検®
- TOEIC®
- 日常学習

▼ユーザー対象
中学生	高校生	大学生	社会人
○	◎	◎	○

▶紹介動画

各種試験に必要な単語・熟語・文法が楽しく身につく！

※各種教材のトレーニング（の一部）、オンライン対戦、フレンド検索機能などがすべて無料でご利用頂けます。

「みんなの一問一答オンライン」の特長

特長1
基礎・基本
学習の「基礎・基本」が楽しく完璧に身につく！

特長2
対戦／フレンド／コメント
みんなとつながる、みんなで学ぶ。

ガリレイ　アインシュタイン

特長3
召喚（ガチャ）／成長進化／キャラ
学習するほどキャラが成長・進化！

吉田松陰

▶ 大学受験や英検・TOEICなどに必要な単語・熟語・文法・用語等の「基礎・基本」が、ゲーム感覚で楽しく身につきます。
「早押しクイズ」形式の**オンライン対戦**で、マスターした知識を全国のユーザーやフレンドと競い合うこともでき、勝てば勝つほど「全国ランキング」が上がります。

▶ 全国のユーザーから同じ志望校や目的を持つ**フレンド**を探すことができます。フレンドどうし、お互いの学習成果を認め合いながら、有意義な情報交換をして受験を有利に進めましょう。
また、1つ1つの問題についてユーザー全員が**コメント**を投稿・閲覧できます。みんなで一緒に学力を高めましょう。

▶ 動物の**星霊**や歴史的な**偉人**のキャラが「守護神（学習コーチ）」となって学習をリードしてくれます。そして、学習すればするほど、キャラも成長・進化します。学習すると獲得できるチケットでキャラを**召喚**しましょう。偉人は進化するたびに**偉人伝**が段階的に読めるようになります。

東進ブックスのベストセラーがゲームで学べる！

学習教材一覧
日本史一問一答	【90万部発行】
古文単語 400	【25万部発行】
英検®準2級英単語 1000	
英検®2級英単語 1400	
TOEIC®英単語 基礎 1500	
TOEIC®英単語 必修 1500	
一億人の英文法	【69万部発行】
一億人の英会話	
英熟語 1000	【10万部発行】

ぞくぞく追加予定

※2022年5月現在。学習教材は予告なく変更になる場合がございますので、あらかじめご了承ください。

基本プレイ無料キャンペーン中！
※教材の全範囲が利用可能になる「有料版」は現在準備中です。詳細が決まり次第、下記HPにて発表いたしますので、どうぞお楽しみに！

まずは無料体験からニャ！

動作環境
スマホ／タブレット／PC Win/Mac

【推奨WEBブラウザ・バージョン】
Google Chrome・91以降／Microsoft Edge・91以降／Safari・15以降

詳しくはHPで▶ みんなの一問一答　検索

株式会社ナガセ 出版事業部
〈お問い合わせ〉minna1q1a@toshin.com

東進ブックス

Seize the Day!
Translation [和訳]

Seize the Day!

和訳

これは実話に基づいたフィクションである。

Chapter 1 *Prologue*

プロローグ

　奥田ダイキは、難関大学を受験しようという学生たちに日本文学を教えている。彼は日本の予備校界のトップ講師の一人だ。彼は日本最大級の権威ある予備校の一つ、特進セミナーで教鞭をとっている。彼はまた、塾、つまり個人経営の小さな学校も所有している。彼は何十冊もの本を書いてきたが、それらは学生にも社会人にも大変人気がある。

　「だからな、よく聞け。自分で時々そう思ってもな、お前はバカじゃない。諦めなければ何だってできるんだよ。いいか、自分を信じるんだぞ」彼は生徒たちにいつもこう言う。その言葉はとても勇気を与えるものだ。

　多くの学生たちがこの言葉に励まされ、彼の勉強法を実践し、劇的に点数を伸ばして入学試験に合格した。それだけでなく、多くの生徒は、大学に合格して仕事を始めた後もその言葉を守り続ける。多くの生徒が目標を達成し、今では医者や弁護士、企業のオーナーとして働いている。

　ダイキは多くのエリートを教え、育ててきたのだ。しかし、彼自身はそうではなかった。

　これは、彼の人生の物語だ。

Chapter 2 *Daiki the Prodigy*

天才よいこちゃんダイキ

奥田ダイキは 1966 年、横浜の郊外の大船で生まれた。彼は優しく、愛情に溢れた両親に育てられた。彼の父は銀行で働き、母は生命保険の販売をしていた。彼には一つ年下のセイジロウという弟がいた。ダイキは他の子供よりも早く話し始め、明らかに賢い子供だった。

幼稚園では、先生たちによく神童と呼ばれた。ダイキは先生に褒められるのが好きで、よく自発的に教室の片付けをしたり、他の子供たちが読んだ後置きっ放しにした本を片付けたりした。

小学校の成績は全ての科目で優れており、両親がダイキに難関中学を受験させようとしたのは自然なことだった。ダイキもまた、合格するのは当然だと思った。

日本で義務教育は、15歳まで続く。そしてほとんどの生徒は、15歳まで公立の学校に通う。しかし優秀な学生の何人かは、トップ大学に生徒を大勢合格させる高校に附属した難関中学校の試験を受ける。これがいわゆる「エリートコース」だ。

4年生になると、ダイキは塾に通い入試のための勉強を始めた。彼はそこでの成績も優秀だった。彼には、同じ小学校に通うマコトという名前のライバルがいた。生まれながらの天才で、最小限の努力で良い点を取ることができたダイキと違い、マコトは生活の全てを勉強にあてて、何とかダイキに追いつくことができていた。ダイキはマコトのことをあまり気にかけていなかったが、マコトはダイキやダイキのテストの結果をいつも気にしていた。二人とも光栄中学を受験することになっていた。

数ヶ月が過ぎ、ついに光栄中学の合格発表の日がやってきた。寒い日

Seize the Day!

和訳

だった。ダイキは合格者名が掲示されるのを待っていた。ついに合格者名が掲示板に掲げられた時、ダイキは自分の受験番号を探した。思った通りだった。彼は自分の番号を見つけることができなかったのだ。

Chapter 3 *The Reason*

理由

もちろん彼の失敗には理由があった。

ダイキは試験の直前にひどい風邪にかかったのだ。薬を飲んだものの、試験の日の朝、熱は三十八度を超えており、薬のせいで頭はぼーっとしていた。とても難関校の試験を受けられる状態ではなかった。

ダイキは何もせずに諦めたくなかったので、とにかくテストを受けることにした。彼がテストを受けた時は、目を開けているのがやっとの状態だった。普段の半分の力も、発揮することができなかった。家に帰った後はすぐに寝込んでしまい、翌日の午後2時まで目覚めることがなかった。

発表の日、試験の不合格を知っても、彼は一緒にいた母に何の言い訳もしなかった。ダイキと母が帰途につくと、マコトとその母親に出会った。

マコトはダイキに言った。「やあ、ダイキ。やったよ。合格したよ。一緒に光栄で勉強できるね。新しい生活、楽しもうね」

ダイキと母は彼の言葉に応えることができなかった。ぎこちない沈黙が少し続き、マコトは直感的にダイキが失敗したのだと分かり「あ、ごめん。もしかして…」と言った。

「心配するなよ。運が悪かっただけさ。マコト、おめでとう。努力が

実ったな」ダイキは何とか作り笑いをして言った。

「本当に気の毒だったね。君は公立に行っても大丈夫だと思うよ。君の頭脳があれば、何だってできるさ」マコトは同情した顔つきで言った。しかし、マコトの暗い表情に反して、マコトの口角が少し上がっているのがダイキの目に入った。それを見た時、ダイキは今まで感じたことがないほど惨めな気持ちになった。世界はいかに不平等なのか、という感覚が込み上げてきた。

ダイキが家に戻った時、セイジロウが彼のことを待っていた。セイジロウはダイキが試験の日にとても調子が悪かったのを知っていたので、結果を尋ねなかった。セイジロウはただ微笑んで、兄を家に迎え入れた。ダイキも彼に微笑んで言った。「心配するなよ。俺は大丈夫だから。おい、トランプでもやるか？　2階に行こうぜ」セイジロウも微笑み、二人は自分たちの部屋に行った。

Chapter 4 *Daiki and Jun*

ダイキとジュン

そのようないきさつで、ダイキは公立中学に入学することになった。彼は入学式に出たくなかった。小学校時代の友達に会い、光栄中学の入試に失敗したことを説明したくなかったのだ。もう何を学ぼうという気も起こらなかったので、学校に行きたいとは全く思わなかった。ダイキは勉強することを嫌悪し始めた。勉強が彼を惨めにしたと思い込んだからだ。

入学式でダイキは、彼が入試に合格したかなど、全く気にかけていないような大勢の友人と出会った。

Seize the Day!

和訳

ダイキの旧友のジュンは言った。「おい、お前落ちたんだってな。残念だったな。でもこれでお前と3年間一緒に過ごせるから、実は俺、嬉しいんだよ。本当のことを言うとな、お前と話ができなくなるのは残念だなって思っていたんだよ」

ダイキはそれを聞いて感激した。そして同時に、ジュンや多くの旧友と別れるのを当然だと考えていたことが、恥ずかしくなった。彼は学校で良い成績を取るより、友達の方がずっと大事だということに気付いたのだ。

ジュンはとても背が高く、髪は短い縮れ毛だった。彼は直情的な性格で、とても短気だった。幼い頃から、彼はいつも問題を起こしていた。彼は怒ると、感情を抑えることが全くできなかった。

入学式が終わり、ジュンとダイキが校門に向かって一緒に歩いていると、三人の少年が彼らを取り囲んだ。少年たちは、新入生には見えなかった。三人とも背が高かった。

「よう、元気か。俺たち、ちょっと金に困ってるんだ。助けてくれねえか？ 少し貸してくれよ」一番体の大きな少年が笑いながら話しかけてきたが、言い方は脅迫そのものだった。ダイキの心臓はドキドキし始めた。彼はどうすれば良いのか、分からなかった。この状況を切り抜けるには、いくらかお金を渡すしかないと彼は考えていた。

ダイキが気が付かないうちに、ジュンが一番背の高い少年に向かって走り出した。そして背中を反らせて拳を握り、全力でその少年を殴った。ジュンはその少年の不意を突き、真正面から顔を殴った。少年は地面に倒れ、鼻から血が流れた。そしてジュンは少年を激しく蹴り始めた。残る二人の少年は凍り付き、動くことができなかった。地面に血が広がった。「止めてくれ。ごめんなさい。ごめんなさい」そう言って少年は泣きながら懇願したが、ジュンは少年が気を失うまで止めなかった。

和訳

　ダイキと二人の少年は、ただ立って見ているしかなかった。ダイキはジュンが少し怖くなったが、同時に、ジュンをとてもかっこいいと思った。ダイキは、今まで感じたことのない、ある種の興奮を感じていた。

　彼は、自分もジュンと同じような強さを身につけたいと思った。

　後で分かったことだが、ジュンがやっつけた少年は、番長だった。

Chapter 5 *Kenji*

ケンジ

　ダイキは全く勉強しなかった。ほんの少しも、だ。彼は勉強を嫌悪した。教室で、彼はただ寝ているか漫画を読んでいた。もちろん時々、先生は彼を叱りつけたが、彼は先生を無視するか、教室を出て、同じクラスになったジュンと散歩に出かけた。彼らはいつも一緒にいた。彼らは校舎の裏でタバコを吸い、読んでいた漫画の内容について語り合った。

　その頃、ダイキとジュンは、全校の生徒と教師の間で番長をやっつけた奴らだと、有名になっていた。彼らに話しかけたり、気にかけたりする者は多くなかった。彼らは、やりたいことはほとんど何でも好き勝手にできた。

　そんな風に１年が過ぎると、ダイキは退屈し始めた。ある日、ダイキとジュンが歩いていると、学校の近くに空手道場があるのに気が付いた。面白そうだったので、彼らは中に入った。

　そこでは、数人の少年が稽古をしていた。少年たちは、高校生と中学生のようだった。先生はがっしりした体格の男性だった。彼らは互いに試合をするのではなく、型の練習をしていた。その様子は、まるで踊っているように見えた。それを見ながら、ダイキとジュンは笑った。彼ら

135

Seize the Day!

和訳

はそこにいる全員に聞こえるようにとても大きな声で笑った。

一人の少年が動きを止め、二人に向かって言った。「おかしいと思うか。ここはお前らのような弱虫が来る場所じゃない。出て行け」彼は背が低く、髪は短かった。彼は先生と同じようにがっしりした体格だった。

彼の言葉を聞くと、ジュンが彼に向かって突進した。ダイキは、ジュンがいつものように少年をやっつけるだろうと思った。ジュンはいつも最初の一撃で敵を倒した。ジュンはいつも通り体を反らせて、拳を全力で前に突き出した。ダイキは「決まった！」と思った。

だが、少年は簡単にパンチをよけると、ジュンの背中にチョップを入れた。ジュンは床の上にうつ伏せに倒れた。ジュンは立ち上がり、咳をすると、もう一度少年に向かって突進した。今度は少年の方もジュンに向かって突進し、腰を低くして、ジュンの腹に強いパンチを食らわせた。

ジュンは床を転げ回り、あえぎながら「殺してやる…」と言った。

「そうか、できるならやってみろ。どうした、これで終わりか？」と、少年は言った。

Chapter 6 *Karate*

空手

ジュンは立ち上がったが、ヨロヨロふらついていた。彼は再び拳を振り上げた。彼がもう一発パンチを放とうとした時、少年は彼の腹に蹴りを入れた。ジュンは一瞬空中を飛び、大きな音を立てて床に落ちた。彼はノックアウトされたのだ。

ダイキは呆然と立ち尽くし、一言も話すことができなかった。ダイキが地元で最強だと思っていたジュンより、少年の方がはるかに強かった

のだ。

「おい、お前。こいつを起こすのを手伝ってくれ。行くぞ」少年はダイキに声をかけた。

ダイキは何も言わずに、少年がジュンを部屋の隅に運ぶのを手伝った。先生と他の生徒たちは彼らを見ていた。少年が先生に言った。「先生、しばらくこいつの面倒を見てもいいかな」先生はうなずいた。

少年はジュンの頭の下に枕を置き、ダイキに様子を見てくれと頼んだ。彼はその場を離れると、濡れタオルを持って戻ってきた。少年がジュンの額にタオルを乗せると、ジュンは目を開けた。怒りの表情は消えていた。

少年はジュンに言った。「いい勝負だったな。お前の力があれば、すごい空手選手になれるぜ。ここで空手を習えよ」ジュンは何も話さず、うなずいた。

「名前は？」と、ダイキが尋ねた。

「ケンジ。大倉ケンジだ。ケンジって呼んでくれ」

彼らが話していると、先生が怒った声で言った。「お前たち、何をしている。ケンジは稽古に戻れ。それからそっちの二人は、入門する気があるなら、道着に着替えてこい。更衣室に予備があるからな」

こうしてダイキとジュンは空手を習い始めた。ケンジは、ダイキとジュンと同学年の中学生だった。

稽古の後、ダイキとジュンとケンジは道場を出た。すると道場の前に、窓にスモークを貼った大きな黒いセダンが停まっていた。サングラスをかけたヤクザのような男が運転席に座り、彼らを見ていた。

Seize the Day!
和訳

Chapter 7 *Motorcycle Gang*

暴走族

P.46　ケンジが男に声をかけた。「兄貴、迎えに来てくれてありがとう。こいつらは俺の新しい友達で、ジュンとダイキだ」

「そうか。乗りな」ケンジの兄がそう言うと、三人は後部座席に乗り込んだ。エンジンがうなり、ロックの曲が大音量で流れていた。ダイキとジュンは、この男と車をかっこいいと思った。

P.47　ダイキとジュンは全く勉強せず、部活にも入っていなかったので、彼らが学んでいたのは空手だけだった。彼らは毎日道場に通い、熱心に練習した。彼らは強くなりたかった——ケンジと同じくらい強く。

1年半が過ぎた。ダイキとジュンとケンジは、いつも一緒に行動していた。その頃には、三人は市で最も強い空手選手になっていた。彼らは何度もケンカをして、地元のたくさんの不良をやっつけていた。今や彼らの名前は、横浜地域中に知れ渡っていた。

P.48　ケンジはダイキやジュンとは違う中学校に通っていたが、二人と同じように勉強はしていなかった。この頃、三人はどこの高校に進学するか決めなければならなかったが、彼らには一つしか選択肢がなかった。成開高校だ。全く人気のない私立学校で、誰でも入学できたため、多くの不良たちがこの学校に通っていた。

三人は成開高校に入学した。そこでも、彼らは毎日ケンカばかりしていた。

P.50　三人全員が16歳になると、バイクの免許を取るために、彼らは教習所に通うことにした。免許を取るためには、運転の実習だけでなく、多くの講義に出席し、最終試験に合格しなければならなかった。授業で居眠りをすると、単位をもらえなかった。彼らはどうしても免許が欲し

かったので、全ての授業に出席した。だが、ジュンとケンジは最終試験に合格できなかった。ダイキは簡単に合格した。彼は試験に向けて準備はしなかったが、授業の内容の記憶だけで、試験に合格するには充分だった。

ジュンとケンジは、ダイキにどうやって試験勉強をすれば良いのか尋ねた。そこで、ダイキは彼らに教え始めた。ダイキは彼らに情報の覚え方と問題の解き方を教えた。彼は、中学入試に向けて準備している時に、こうした技術を身につけていたのだ。

二人はダイキの教え方に感心した。彼は難しい概念を、分かりやすく教えることができた。彼は二人が理解できるたとえや比喩を使い、退屈してくると、内容に関係する冗談を言った。ダイキのおかげで、次の試験では、彼らは簡単に合格した。免許を取ると、三人は当然のように地元の暴走族に入った。

暴走族のメンバーは、バイクにさまざまな飾りを付けて自分好みに改造したり、エンジン音を大きくするためにマフラーを外したりしていた。彼らは、誰もに注目されるように道路を集団で走っていた。それは、不良少年が一般の人々に存在を認めてもらうための方法だった。

暴走族は少年の不良行為の一つで、1970年代から80年代の日本ではどこでも見られるものだった。通常16歳から20歳の少年たちで構成されており、非常によく組織化されていた。どの暴走族でも厳しい上下関係があり、メンバーには個別に役割と階級が与えられ、厳格に守られていた。

ある日、ダイキとジュンとケンジは、暴走族の総長に呼び出された。特定のメンバーが指名され、呼び出されるのは、たいてい重大な用件がある時だった。三人は午前0時に港に来るように言われた。ダイキは一体何があるのだろうかと思った。

Seize the Day!
和訳

　彼らが港に着くと、何人かの幹部連中が彼らに岸壁の端に立つよう指示した。彼らがまっすぐ並んで立つと、突然黒い大きなセダンが彼らに向かって走り寄ってきた。

Chapter 8 *Corruption*

堕落の果て

P.56

　ダイキとジュンとケンジは岸壁の端に立ち、彼らに向かって加速する黒いセダンを見ていた。彼らは身動き一つしなかった。空手の先生は、彼らに敵が来ても絶対にひるむなと話していた。彼らは先生の教えを守ったのだ。セダンは急ブレーキの音を立てて彼らの目の前で止まり、暴走族の総長が車から出てきた。彼は大柄で恰幅の良い男で、髪にはパー

P.58

マをかけ、黒い上着を着ていた。「よし。大したもんだ。お前ら根性がありそうだな。お前らはケンカが強いそうだな。これから、お前らに大事な役目を与えるぞ。俺の用心棒になれ。いいな」と、彼は言った。これは特別なことだった。総長の用心棒になるということは、暴走族の中で一目置かれる存在になるということだ。三人はこの仕事を与えられたことを誇りに思い、喜んで引き受けた。

　それから数ヶ月間、彼らは若者が想像できる、あらゆる悪事を経験し

P.59

た。彼らにとって、人生の最盛期だった。ダイキは、自分たちがしていることは間違っていると分かっていたが、自分を抑えることができなかった。結局、彼は周りにいる他の少年たちと同じ行動をとっていただけなのだ。彼は多くの法を犯していることを分かっていたが、気にしなかった。間違っているのは大人や社会の不公平のせいだと、彼は考えていた。

ある夜、彼は家で弟のセイジロウとトランプをしていた。ダイキは、セイジロウと一緒にいる時が、一番気が楽だった。弟と一緒にいると、彼は自分自身を取り戻すことができた。セイジロウはダイキに自分が出会った女の子のことを話し、父親には絶対に聞くことのできない性についての質問をした。ダイキは、兄弟は仲良くなれないと聞いたことがあったが、信じられなかった。彼は、彼とセイジロウは世界で一番仲の良い兄弟だと思っていた。

　突然、下の階から、母親が彼らを呼ぶ声が聞こえた。彼女はダイキにお客さんが来ていると言った。ダイキが下に降りると、黒いスーツを着た二人の男性がいた。彼らは言った。「君がこれまで起こした事件のことで、君を警察に連行しないといけない。証拠は全て揃っているから、何も言わずに、一緒に来なさい」母親は泣いていた。セイジロウは階段の上から様子を見ていた。彼の目には涙が溢れていた。

Chapter 9 *Juvenile Corrective Institution*

少年鑑別所

　ダイキはセイジロウに別れを告げたかったが、警官は彼にその機会を与えなかった。彼らはダイキの腕をつかんで家から連れ出し、待機していたパトカーに乗せた。

　ダイキは、警察の留置場で数日過ごした。何回かの尋問と短い審判の後、当局はダイキを少年鑑別所に送ることを決定した。

　ダイキは少年鑑別所に夜、到着した。少し面談をした後、彼は部屋へと連れて行かれた。少年鑑別所では、1つの部屋を6人で使用する。ダイキが部屋に入ると、残りの5人が彼をにらみつけた。ダイキは何も言

Seize the Day!
和訳

わなかった。彼は5人をにらみ返した。

就寝時間になり、照明が消えた。ダイキが布団に入ると、枕を顔に強く押しつけられた。腕と脚は二人の少年によって押さえつけられていた。ダイキは逃げようとしたが、少しも動くことができなかった。

突然、ダイキは腹に鋭い痛みを感じた。誰かが彼を蹴飛ばしたのだ。蹴りは続いていた。誰も一言も話さなかった。ダイキが逃げるのを諦めるまで、少年たちは代わる代わる彼を蹴り続けた。

翌朝、ダイキが起き上がると、体中に激しい痛みを感じた。他の少年たちは彼をあざ笑っていた。ダイキは怒りを感じたが、その時は何かしたり言ったりはしなかった。彼は立つのもやっとだったが、全ての日課をこなした。夜になり、また照明が消えた。

今度はダイキも準備をしていた。彼は目を開けたまま横になっていたのだ。

少年たちが彼の方に来る音を聞くと、彼は立ち上がった。彼の目は暗闇に慣れていたので、彼には少年たちの居場所が分かった。

ダイキは目の前の少年を蹴った。少年は小さくうめき声をあげた。それから、ダイキは彼の腹を思い切り殴り、彼を倒した。他の少年たちが一斉にダイキに向かってきたが、ダイキは勝てる相手ではなかった。1分もしないうちに、ダイキは全員をやっつけた。

翌日から、少年たちのダイキに対する態度は完全に変わった。彼らはとても友好的になったのだ。彼らにとって、ダイキのような者が同じ集団にいると、他の集団に対して非常に有利になるのだった。

ダイキは他の集団の少年と何度かケンカをしたが、いつも相手を負かした。彼は、看守に捕まらないよう、細心の注意を払っていた。彼は、相手の顔は攻撃しなかった。顔に跡が残れば、看守にケンカをしたことがばれたからだ。そんなふうに数週間が過ぎ、ダイキは彼の刑期が終わ

ったと告げられた。ダイキが少年鑑別所を出所する日、朝食後に、看守が他の少年たち全員にダイキが出所すると話した。少年たちは次々に立ち上がり、ダイキに向かって頭を下げた。少年たちの多くは、ダイキの性格やケンカの技が大好きだった。

その時急に一人の看守が食堂に駆け込み、ダイキに急いで荷造りをするように指示した。看守はとても真剣な顔をしていた。ダイキが荷物をまとめると外に連れ出され、パトカーの後部座席に乗るように言われた。パトカーはサイレンを鳴らして発進した。

「何だよ。どうなってんだよ」ダイキは尋ねた。

助手席に乗っていた警官が答えた。「お前の弟がね、事故にあったんだよ」

Chapter 10 *A Sudden Farewell*

突然の別れ

パトカーは大船に着き、交差点で止まった。ダイキが車を降りると、ガソリンとゴムの臭いがした。大型トラックがガードレールに衝突して、ガソリンがしたたり落ちていた。作業員と警官が走り回っていた。ダイキは母親が道路に座って泣いているのを見た。彼女の後ろには弟の自転車が見えたが、めちゃくちゃに潰れていた。

自転車の横に、担架に乗せられたセイジロウが見えた。彼は学校の制服を着ていた。彼は眠っているようだった。いつもより少し小さく見える顔の上に、白い布がかけられていた。

ダイキは弟の方に向かって歩き、そばに立った。彼は自分の見ているものが信じられなかった。あまりに現実離れしていた。彼がしゃがんで、

Seize the Day!

和訳

セイジロウの顔の上の布に手をかけると、警官が彼の手をつかんだ。

「止めておきなさい。私には君を止める権限はないが、見ない方が、君と弟さんのためだ。弟さんは昔の姿じゃない。見るのは止めなさい」

ダイキは道路に座り込み、弟の手を握った。手は冷たかった。涙が顔を流れ落ちた。

事故が起きた時、セイジロウは自転車で登校するところだった。トラックの運転手はよそ見をしていて、赤信号で止まらなかった。警察の説明では、セイジロウは、跳ねられて即死したということだった。

事故の後の数日間、ダイキと両親はセイジロウの葬儀の手配や、地元の報道機関への記者への対応に追われた。悲しむ時間はあまりなかった。

全てが片付いた時、彼らは疲れ切っていた。彼らには、話をしたり、どこかに出かけたりする気力は残っていなかった。ダイキは数日間、自分の部屋で過ごした。

ダイキがベッドに横たわり、天井を見つめていると、突然誰かがドアをノックした。ジュンだった。ケンジも一緒だった。彼らは黒いツナギを着ていた。彼らはダイキの腕をつかみ、「行くぞ」と言った。

「どこへ」ダイキは尋ねた。

「聞くな。とにかくバイクに乗って、ついてくりゃいいんだ」と、二人は答えた。

Chapter 11 *The Last Run*

最後の暴走

11月の寒い夜だった。空には雲一つなく、星が明るく輝いていた。彼らは遊園地の巨大な駐車場に着いた。何百人もの暴走族のメンバーが

和訳

待っていた。彼らは全員黒いツナギを着ていた。彼らのバイクのエンジンは、うなりを上げていた。

暴走族の総長は、ダイキに先頭を走るように命じた。それはメンバーにとって最大の名誉だった。総長はダイキに言った、「俺たちはみな、お前の弟に起きた悲劇を知ってる。これは、お前とお前の弟の魂に敬意を払うための俺たちなりのやり方だ。この走りが終わったら、族を抜けるかどうかはお前が決めればいい。今夜は全部忘れて、富士スピードウェイまで一緒に走るぞ」

横浜周辺の暴走族は、年に数回、横浜のある場所に集まって、富士山を目指して走っていた。ゴールは富士スピードウェイという自動車レース場の駐車場だった。特に大晦日には、横浜と周辺の地域の多くの暴走族が合流して、数千人で富士山を目指したものだった。警察に妨害されるため、彼らが目的地にたどり着くことはまずなかった。彼らはたいてい警察に捕まるか、引き返していた。それでも彼らにとって、富士スピードウェイにたどり着くことは夢だった。

時間は深夜二時近かった。暴走族は、ダイキを先頭に走り始めた。不思議なことに、その夜は警察の妨害を受けなかった。横浜を出る前に、他の暴走族が合流した。その時点で仲間は千人を超えていた。静岡県に入ると、何台かのパトカーが後ろに現れた。暴走族に対し拡声器で指示する声が聞こえた。「止まれ。今すぐ止まりなさい。さもないと逮捕するぞ」

最後尾を走っていたメンバーが速度を落とし、パトカーの前に止まって、他のメンバーを先に行かせた。さらに多くのパトカーが来たが、また他のメンバーが犠牲になり、ダイキの集団が走り続けられるようにした。

ようやく、ダイキたちは富士スピードウェイの駐車場に入った。ダイ

Seize the Day!
和訳

キの暴走族がゴールに着いたのは初めてだった。

　時間は6時になっていた。ダイキとジュンとケンジは美しい日の出を見ながら、バイクに座って話していた。その朝、三人は暴走族を卒業して、大人になることを決めた。

Chapter 12 *Daiki and Yumi*

ダイキとユミ

P.88　ダイキとジュンとケンジは、高校生としての普通の生活に戻った。学校の先生が、彼らが授業にきちんと出席すれば、卒業には問題ないだろうと言ったので、彼らは毎日学校に通った。もっとも、他の生徒と同様に授業中は寝ているか、漫画を読んでいたのだが。

　高校の卒業式の日、駅から家に帰る途中で、ダイキは少女が不良少年

P.89　に囲まれているのを見た。彼女が着ていた制服から、彼には彼女が横浜の一流高校の1つである山下高校の生徒だと分かった。彼女は黒くまっすぐな髪をしていた。彼女は美しい目をしていたが、目には涙がたまっていた。

　ダイキは少女に向かって歩き、少年たちをにらんで言った。「俺は成開高校の奥田ダイキだ。お前ら、初めて見る顔だな。一緒に楽しむか」

P.90　奥田ダイキという名前を聞いて、少年たちは青ざめた。恐怖で震えている者もいた。彼らの一人が言った。「いや、彼女に駅までどうやって行くか教えていただけです。初めまして。あなたの噂はよく聞いています。失礼します。もう行かないと。じゃあ」

　少年たちが去った後、少女がダイキに話しかけた。「助けてくれてありがとう。私はユミ。山本ユミよ。あなたの名前はダイキね」そう言う

と、彼女はダイキの目を見つめた。

　ダイキはたくさんの女の子と付き合ってきたが、これほど胸がドキドキするのは初めてだった。彼の顔は赤くなった。そんな彼を見て、ユミは微笑んで言った。「コーヒーをおごって、恥ずかしがり屋さん」

　こうして、ダイキとユミは付き合い始めた。高校を卒業すると、ダイキは中古車のセールスマンになり、ユミは大学に進学した。彼女はアルバイトでファッションモデルの仕事もしていた。彼らは小さなアパートで一緒に暮らし始めた。

　ジュンはパチンコ屋で働き始め、ケンジは兄と同じヤクザになった。彼らはそれぞれ自分の道を歩み、一緒に会うことは少なくなっていった。

　働き始めて最初の数ヶ月、ダイキの収入は月8万円しかなかったのに対し、ユミはアルバイトでその倍を稼いでいた。ダイキはユミを心から愛しており、ユミも同じように愛してくれていると信じていた。彼は、彼女に見合う人間になれるよう懸命に働いた。ダイキは毎日夜遅くまで働いていた。彼は、ユミが彼のために作る食事と1杯のビールを楽しみに、いつも10時過ぎに家に帰っていた。

　ある日、彼がアパートに帰ると、ユミはいなくなっていて、彼女の荷物もなくなっていた。ダイキはテーブルに置いてあるメモを見つけた。

Chapter 13 *He's Different from You.*

彼はあなたと違うの

　メモにはこう書いてあった。「ダイキ、あなたがとてもいい人なのは分かっているけど、私にはあなたと一緒の将来が想像できないの。ごめんなさい。私を探さないで。

Seize the Day!

和訳

　　さようなら。ユミ」
　　ダイキは前日にユミが言ったことを思い出した。「不安だわ。私たちの将来が心配なの。私が夢見ていた生活とは全然違う。これ以上あなたを愛せるかどうか分からない」そう言いながら、彼女は泣いていた。
　　ダイキは、彼女が出て行ったのはお金のせいだと思った。彼は、彼女を取り戻すためには、もっとたくさん稼ぐ必要があると考えた。彼は、会社でトップのセールスマンになったら彼女を探して会おうと決めた。
　　彼は、ただ必死に働くだけでは足りないと思った。彼は営業の技術に関する本を買って勉強した。また、他のセールスマンが車を売る方法を観察した。彼は、新しい顧客を見つけるより、既に持っている人脈を活かすことが、車を売る上で非常に重要だということに気付いた。
　　ダイキは、暴走族時代の仲間全員に電話をかけた。彼らの大部分が車の免許を取ったばかりで、車を買おうとしていた。
　　彼らは喜んでダイキから車を買ってくれた。中には、ダイキから新しい車を買うために、古い車を売ってくれた者までいた。
　　たった2ヶ月で、ダイキは会社でトップのセールスマンになった。彼の月給は跳ね上がった。さらに社長の平沢さんから特別ボーナスまでもらった。
　　ダイキはユミを探して電話をすることにした。多くの友達に尋ねて、ようやくユミの電話番号が分かり、彼女に電話をかけた。
　　「やあ、ユミ。いろいろと心配をかけて悪かったな。俺たちの将来についてのお前の気持ちは良く分かる。だけど、問題は解決したんだ。俺は会社でトップのセールスマンになったし、平沢さんは来月から35万円払うって約束してくれたんだよ。50万円の特別ボーナスまでもらったんだ。お祝いをしよう。何がしたい。何が食べたい。何でも言ってくれ」と、ダイキは言った。

ユミはこう答えた。「違うの、ダイキ。あなたは分かってない。そんなことが問題じゃないの。別のことなのよ。あのね…実は私、他の人に出会ったの。彼もアルバイトでモデルをしていて、私、その人と付き合っているの」

「何だって。他の奴と付き合っている？ どういうことだよ。そいつのどこが特別だっていうんだよ。俺じゃ不満なのか。なぜだよ、ユミ」

「そうね。彼はあなたとは違うの。彼、とても頭がいいのよ。大学でね、法律を勉強しているの。彼、セイト大学に通っているのよ。弁護士になるって言っているわ。とにかく…ごめんなさい。もう電話しないで」彼女は電話を切った。

Chapter 14 I'll Show Them.

やってやるぜ！

ユミの言葉に、ダイキは自分が全く価値のない人間なのだと感じた。彼は合格発表の日のマコトの表情や、自分が中学校で先生たちにどんな扱いを受けてきたかを思い出した。そして、彼の心の中で何かがはじけた。

彼はもう一度やってみることに決めた。彼は受験勉強をすることにしたのだ。

それは彼が大学に行きたかったからではなかった。社会の不公平に対する、彼なりの戦い方だった。学校の成績や一流の仕事がそんなに大事なら、手に入れてやる、全部自分のものにしてやる、と彼は思った。翌朝、彼は平沢さんに辞表を提出した。

平沢さんは理由を聞くと、ダイキを引き止めようとはしなかった。そ

Seize the Day!

和訳

れどころか、彼を励ましてくれた。

ダイキは20歳で、もう12月になっていた。

試験までは2ヶ月ちょっとしか残っていなかった。彼は入試の科目として、英語と国語と日本史を選んだ。

ダイキの作戦は、中学入試の前に持っていた知識を復活させるというものだった。日本では、難関中学の入試は非常に難しいのだ。

一部は大学入試と同じくらい難しいものもある。ダイキは、小学生の頃、塾で学んだものを思い出すことから始めた。1ヶ月後、彼は国語と日本史ではかなり良い成績を取れるようになった。これら2科目の模試の得点は、求められる水準を超えていた。

しかし、英語はどうすれば良いか分からなかった。彼は、英語の授業が始まる中学に入学した時点で勉強を止めてしまっていたので、"you"や"them"のような簡単な単語の読み方すら知らなかった。彼は英語の低い得点を補うため、残りの2科目に集中することにした。そのためには、2科目で90パーセント以上を取る必要があった。彼に、無駄にできる時間はなかった。

一月の中旬になった。ダイキにとって、最初の入試のちょうど1ヶ月前だった。成人の日の前日、彼はジュンから電話をもらった。

日本では、その学年に20歳になる人のために、市が成人式を実施する。ジュンは、式の後に多くの旧友が大きなパーティーを開くと話し、ダイキにも参加して欲しいと言った。

ダイキは成人式に出席する予定だったが、終わったらすぐ家に帰って勉強しようと思っていた。彼は時間を無駄にしたくなかったのだ。同時に、彼は旧友に会いたいと心から思った。

彼の中では、ストレスを解消するために、一晩だけパーティーに行ってもかまわないという気持ちもあった。

ところが突然ダイキはナイフを手に机から立ち上がり、母親が成人式のために用意したスーツを切り裂き始めた。一着しかないスーツを台無しにしたため、これで彼は式にも出席できなくなった。彼は涙を流していた。

Chapter 15 *Is This My Mission in Life?*

俺の人生の目標？

ダイキは1日たりとも休まなかった。彼は1日に3時間から5時間しか眠らなかった。最初の試験の日まで、そんな日々が続いた。最初の入試は学国大学の入試だった。ダイキの第一志望校だ。学国大学は日本文学の研究で有名な大学で、ダイキは、この大学で古典を学びたいと思っていたのだ。

最初の科目は英語だった。彼はできるだけのことはしたが、ほとんどの問題を間違えたことは分かっていた。彼は気にしなかった。彼の予想どおりだったからだ。

次の科目は国語だった。ダイキは90パーセント以上の問題に正解したと思った。3番目の科目は日本史だ。試験が始まった時、ダイキは嬉しくて叫びそうになった。ほとんどの問題が、彼が一週間前に勉強した内容とそっくりだったのだ。彼は試験に合格することを確信した。彼の予想は正しかった。彼は学国大学の入試に合格した。それだけでなく、他に受験した大学も全て合格した。

学国大学に入学するとダイキは日本文学の勉強を始め、そして塾で国語と日本史を教え始めた。彼の授業は生徒たちにとても人気があった。すぐに彼は塾でトップの教師になった。ダイキは教えることが大好きで、

Seize the Day!
和訳

生徒たちも愛していた。彼は教えることの力を知った。彼は自分の言葉が生徒たちを励まし、人生を変えることに驚いた。この仕事を通じて、彼は、かつての自分と同じように葛藤する多くの少年少女を救えると確信していた。

彼の指導技術に感心した塾長は、ダイキに卒業したら予備校の講師になることを勧めた。そこでダイキは、特進セミナーの試験を受けることにした。

特進セミナーは日本最大の予備校で、講師は教育業界の中で最高級と見なされている。採用試験に合格できるのは、数百人のうち一人だけだ。

ダイキは試験に合格した。合格しただけではなく、特進セミナーで史上最高の得点を取った。

Chapter 16 *Stairs*

階段

採用試験に合格したという結果を受け取った日、彼は横浜で平沢さんと夕食を食べた。平沢さんは、久しぶりにダイキに会えたことをとても喜んでいた。彼らは夕食を共にし、長時間、話をした。

平沢さんはダイキを送ってやると言い、ダイキを助手席に乗せると、大船に向けて出発した。

突然の出来事だった。ダイキは何が起こったのか分からなかった。彼は体が宙に浮かんでいるような感じがした。振り返ると、平沢さんと自分の姿が見えた。二人とも血まみれになっていた。彼は夢を見ているのだと思ったが、その夢はまるで現実のようだった。

彼の前に、上に登って行く階段が見えた。ダイキはゆっくりと階段を

登り始めた。もう少しで頂上というところで、信じられないものが見えた。

彼がそこで見たのは、弟のセイジロウだったのだ。セイジロウはダイキに笑いかけたが、目には涙が溢れていた。彼らはしばらくの間お互いを見つめていた。涙がダイキの頬を流れ落ちた。

ダイキは手を伸ばして弟に触れようとしたが、ダイキの手がセイジロウの体に触れそうになった時、セイジロウはダイキを強く押した。ダイキは階段の下まで転がり落ちた。

ダイキは病院のベッドで目覚めた。彼は、平沢さんが運転中に眠ってしまい、車がガードレールに衝突して転倒したと聞いた。二人とも、2日間、昏睡状態だった。

退院後、ダイキは特進セミナーで教え始めた。彼は教えることを楽しみ、人生で出会った全ての人、特に弟に感謝した。

ダイキには、階段の頂上で弟が言いたかったことが分かってきた。セイジロウは、ダイキに生きて欲しい、そして素晴らしい人生を楽しんで欲しいと考えていたことを、ダイキは、今、理解していた。

Chapter 17　Believe in Yourself, Okay?

お前はバカじゃない！

奥田ダイキはもう25年以上教鞭をとっている。彼はいつも生徒にこう言う。「人生には、いろんなことが起こるよ。時々うまくいかなくて、間違うことだってある。俺がしたみたいに大きく間違うことだってな。でもな、覚えとけよ。お前たちはいつだって変わることができるんだよ。生きているってのは、すばらしいよ。生きていることに感謝しろよ。一

Seize the Day!
和訳

瞬だって無駄にするんじゃねえ。確かにな、社会ってのは、不公平だよ。人生ってのは不公平なんだよ。でもな、やれば克服できるんだ。だからな、よく聞け。自分で時々そう思ってもな、お前はバカじゃない。諦めなければ、何だってできるんだよ。いいか、自分を信じるんだぞ」

【完】

Seize the Day!
Index [索引]

A

- [ ] **a bit** 熟
[bít] 30
- [ ] **accept** 動
[æksépt] 48, 58
- [ ] **accident** 名
[æksədənt] 70, 75
- [ ] **accomplish** 動
[əkámpliʃ] 20
- [ ] **achieve** 動
[ətʃíːv] 7, 8, 105, 127
- [ ] **actually** 副
[æktʃuəli] 25
- [ ] **a cup of ~** 熟
[kʌ́p] 92
- [ ] **adult** 名
[ədʌ́lt] 85
- [ ] **advantage** 名
[ædvǽntidʒ] 68
- [ ] **advise** 人 to V 熟
[ædváiz] 117
- [ ] **after** (~) 前接
[ǽftər] 8, 90, 93, 99, 116, 120, 124
- [ ] **after all** 熟
[ǽftər] 59
- [ ] **afterwards** 副
[ǽftərwərdz] 109
- [ ] **against ~** 前
[əgénst] 105
- [ ] **a glass of ~** 熟
[glǽs] 93
- [ ] **a kind of ~** 熟
[káind] 30
- [ ] **alike** 副
[əláik] 7
- [ ] **a little** 熟
[lítl] 27, 32, 67, 73, 105
- [ ] **alive** 形
[əláiv] 126
- [ ] **all at once** 熟
[wʌ́ns] 67
- [ ] **all over ~** 熟
[óuvər] 28, 66
- [ ] **all the ~** 熟
[ɔ́ːl] 59, 61, 98, 116
- [ ] **all the way** 熟
[wéi] 123
- [ ] **almost** 副
[ɔ́ːlmoust] 33, 82, 115, 121
- [ ] **a lot** 熟
[lát] 90
- [ ] **a lot of ~** 熟
[lát] 47, 108, 126
- [ ] **also** 副接
[ɔ́ːlsou] 6, 36, 48, 92, 97, 100
- [ ] **although** ..... 接
[ɔːlðóu] 16
- [ ] **amazingly** 副
[əméiziŋli] 11
- [ ] **among ~** 前
[əmʌ́ŋ] 7, 116
- [ ] **amount** 名
[əmáunt] 93
- [ ] **and so** 熟
[ənd sóu] 24
- [ ] **angrily** 副
[ǽŋgrili] 41
- [ ] **angry** 形
[ǽŋgri] 66
- [ ] **announce** 動
[ənáuns] 13
- [ ] **announcement** 名
[ənáunsmənt] 17, 104
- [ ] **answer** 動
[ǽnsər] 70, 77, 100
- [ ] **any** 形
[éni] 96, 109
- [ ] **any more** 熟
[əni mɔ́ːr] 96, 101
- [ ] **anymore** 副
[ènimɔ́ːr] 25
- [ ] **anyone** 代
[éniwʌ̀n] 48
- [ ] **anything** 代
[éniθìŋ] 61, 65, 66, 100, 127
- [ ] **anyway** 副
[éniwèi] 17, 101
- [ ] **apartment** 名
[əpáːrtmənt] 94
- [ ] **appear** 動
[əpíər] 84
- [ ] **area** 名
[ɛ́əriə] 47
- [ ] **around** 副
[əráund] 38
- [ ] **around ~** 前
[əráund] 59
- [ ] **arrange** 動
[əréindʒ] 76
- [ ] **arrest** 動
[ərést] 84
- [ ] **arrive** 動
[əráiv] 13

- [ ] arrive at ~
[əráiv]　　　　　　　　54, 65, 80
- [ ] as ~
[əz]　　　　　　　　　33, 88, 106
- [ ] as .....
[əz]　　　　　　　14, 17, 38, 115
- [ ] as A as B
[əz]　　　　　　　　　　47, 106
- [ ] ashamed .....
[əʃéimd]　　　　　　　　　26
- [ ] ask
[ǽsk]　　　　　21, 41, 60, 70, 77
- [ ] ask 人 to V
[ǽsk]　　　　　　39, 54, 70, 108
- [ ] asleep
[əslí:p]　　　　　　　　　50
- [ ] assign
[əsáin]　　　　　　　　　58
- [ ] as usual
[jú:ʒuəl]　　　　　　　　35
- [ ] as well as A
[wél]　　　　　　　　　　17
- [ ] attend
[əténd]　　　　　　24, 50, 88, 109
- [ ] at the end of ~
[énd]　　　　　　　　　　84
- [ ] at the same time
[táim]　　　　　　　25, 30, 109
- [ ] attitude
[ǽtitjù:d]　　　　　　　　68
- [ ] authority
[əθɔ́:rəti]　　　　　　　　64
- [ ] awake
[əwéik]　　　　　　　　　17
- [ ] awkward
[ɔ́:kwərd]　　　　　　　　19

B

- [ ] back
[bǽk]　　　　　　　　　　35
- [ ] back seat
[bǽk]　　　　　　　　　46, 70
- [ ] backward
[bǽkwərd]　　　　　　　　35
- [ ] badly
[bǽdli]　　　　　　　　　72
- [ ] bank
[bǽŋk]　　　　　　　　　　10
- [ ] barely
[béərli]　　　　　　13, 17, 20, 66
- [ ] be able to V
[éibl]　　　　　　26, 51, 60, 98, 109

- [ ] be about to V
[əbáut]　　　　　　　38, 98, 123
- [ ] be accustomed to ~
[əkʌ́stəmd]　　　　　　　　67
- [ ] beat (~) up (~)
[bí:t]　　　　　30, 33, 35, 47, 68
- [ ] be born
[bɔ́:rn]　　　　　　　　　10
- [ ] be busy Ving
[bízi]　　　　　　　　　　76
- [ ] because .....
[bikɔ́:z]　　　　　　　　24, 110
- [ ] because of ~
[bikɔ́:z]　　　　　　　　82, 97
- [ ] be certain that S V
[sə́:rtn]　　　　　　　　　115
- [ ] be clear from the beginning
[klíər]　　　　　　　　　10
- [ ] become C
[bikʌ́m]　52, 68, 85, 92, 97, 98, 117
- [ ] be composed of ~
[kəmpóuzd]　　　　　　　　53
- [ ] be conscious of ~
[kánʃəs]　　　　　　　　　13
- [ ] be considered C
[kənsídərd]　　　　　　　117
- [ ] be convinced
[kənvínst]　　　　　　　　117
- [ ] be covered in blood
[kʌ́vərd]　　　　　　　　121
- [ ] be different from ~
[dífərənt]　　　　　　　　96
- [ ] be exhausted
[igzɔ́:stid]　　　　　　　　76
- [ ] be famous for ~
[féiməs]　　　　　　　　114
- [ ] before
[bifɔ́:r]　　　　　　　　30, 115
- [ ] be full of ~
[fúl]　　　　　　　　61, 89, 123
- [ ] beg
[bég]　　　　　　　　　　28
- [ ] begin to V
[bigín]　10, 24, 33, 92, 109, 116, 124
- [ ] begin Ving
[bigín]　　　　　　　　　28, 51
- [ ] be glad to V
[glǽd]　　　　　　　　　120
- [ ] behind ~
[biháind]　　　　　　　　32
- [ ] behind the wheel
[hwí:l]　　　　　　　　　42

157

- ☐ be **impressed** by ~ 熟
  [imprést]　117
- ☐ be in no **condition** to V 熟
  [kəndíʃən]　16
- ☐ be in **tears** 熟
  [tíərz]　110
- ☐ **believe** 動
  [bilíːv]　60, 73, 121
- ☐ **believe** in ~ 熟
  [bilíːv]　7, 126
- ☐ **belly** 名
  [béli]　38, 66
- ☐ **belong** to ~ 熟
  [bilɔ́ːŋ]　47
- ☐ **bend** down 熟
  [bénd]　36
- ☐ be no **match** for ~ 熟
  [mætʃ]　67
- ☐ be on one's way **home** 熟
  [hóum]　17
- ☐ be **reluctant** to V 熟
  [rilʌ́ktənt]　24
- ☐ be **scared** of ~ 熟
  [skéərd]　30
- ☐ be **short** of ~ 熟
  [ʃɔ́ːrt]　27
- ☐ **beside** ~ 前
  [bisáid]　73
- ☐ be **similar** to ~ 熟
  [símələr]　115
- ☐ **best** 形
  [bést]　47
- ☐ be **surprised** 熟
  [sərpráizd]　116
- ☐ be **unable** to V 熟
  [ʌnéibl]　28, 38
- ☐ be **up** to ~ 熟
  [ʌ́p]　81
- ☐ be well **known** to ~ 熟
  [nóun]　33
- ☐ **biggest** 形
  [bígəst]　6, 27, 117
- ☐ **bike** 名
  [báik]　75, 77, 85
- ☐ **blush** 動
  [blʌ́ʃ]　92
- ☐ **board** 名
  [bɔ́ːrd]　14
- ☐ **bodyguard** 名
  [bádigàːrd]　58
- ☐ **bonus** 名
  [bóunəs]　98

- ☐ **bored** 形
  [bɔ́ːrd]　33, 52
- ☐ **born** 形
  [bɔ́ːrn]　13
- ☐ **both** 代
  [bóuθ]　121, 124
- ☐ **bow** 動
  [báu]　69
- ☐ **break** 動
  [bréik]　59
- ☐ **brief** 形
  [bríːf]　64
- ☐ **brightly** 副
  [bráitli]　80
- ☐ **bring** up ~ 熟
  [bríŋ]　10
- ☐ **bro** 名
  [bróu]　21, 46
- ☐ **business** 名
  [bíznis]　54

C

- ☐ **call** 動
  [kɔ́ːl]　60, 98, 101
- ☐ **call** O C 熟
  [kɔ́ːl]　11, 41
- ☐ cannot **help** Ving 熟
  [hélp]　20
- ☐ **care** 動
  [kéər]　25, 59, 115
- ☐ **care** about ~ 熟
  [kéər]　33
- ☐ **careful** 形
  [kéərfəl]　68
- ☐ **carefully** 副
  [kéərfəli]　7, 127
- ☐ **carry** 動
  [kǽri]　39
- ☐ **catch** ~ by surprise 熟
  [kǽtʃ]　28
- ☐ **ceiling** 名
  [síːliŋ]　76
- ☐ **celebrate** 動
  [séləbrèit]　100
- ☐ **cell** 名
  [sél]　64
- ☐ **ceremony** 名
  [sérəmòuni]　108
- ☐ **certain** 形
  [sə́ːrtn]　81
- ☐ **chance** 名
  [tʃǽns]　64

158

- ☐ **change** into ~ 熟
  [tʃéindʒ] 42
- ☐ **character** 名
  [kǽriktər] 69
- ☐ **cheek** 名
  [tʃíːk] 123
- ☐ **cheer** ~ on 熟
  [tʃíər] 105
- ☐ **choice** 名
  [tʃɔ́is] 48
- ☐ **choose** 動
  [tʃúːz] 106
- ☐ **chop** 動
  [tʃɑ́p] 35
- ☐ **chore** 名
  [tʃɔ́ːr] 66
- ☐ **class** 名
  [klǽs] 32
- ☐ **clench** 動
  [kléntʃ] 28
- ☐ **climb** into ~ 熟
  [kláim] 46
- ☐ **climb** up the stairs 熟
  [kláim] 121
- ☐ **close** 形
  [klóus] 60
- ☐ **cloth** 名
  [klɔ́ːθ] 73
- ☐ **club** 名
  [kláb] 47
- ☐ **college** 名
  [kɑ́lidʒ] 8, 101, 104
- ☐ **coma** 名
  [kóumə] 124
- ☐ **come** back 熟
  [kám] 39
- ☐ **come** on 熟
  [kám] 36, 39
- ☐ **come** out of ~ 熟
  [kám] 56
- ☐ **come** Ving 熟
  [kám] 54, 69
- ☐ **comic** book 熟
  [kɑ́mik] 32, 88
- ☐ coming-of-age **ceremony** 熟
  [sérəmòuni] 108
- ☐ Coming-of-**Age** Day 熟
  [éidʒ] 108
- ☐ **common** 形
  [kɑ́mən] 53
- ☐ **company** 名
  [kámpəni] 8, 98
- ☐ **comparison** 名
  [kəmpǽrisn] 51
- ☐ **completely** 副
  [kəmplíːtli] 68, 76, 104
- ☐ **compulsory** education 熟
  [kəmpálsəri] 11
- ☐ **concentrate** on ~ 熟
  [kɑ́nsəntrèit] 107
- ☐ **concept** 名
  [kɑ́nsept] 51
- ☐ **Congratulations** 間
  [kəngrætʃuléiʃənz] 19
- ☐ **connection** 名
  [kənékʃən] 97
- ☐ **connected** to ~ 熟
  [kənéktid] 12
- ☐ **constantly** 副
  [kɑ́nstəntli] 26
- ☐ **continue** 動
  [kəntínjuː] 66
- ☐ **control** oneself 熟
  [kəntróul] 59
- ☐ control one's **temper** 熟
  [témpər] 26
- ☐ **cool** 形
  [kúːl] 30, 46
- ☐ **corner** 名
  [kɔ́ːrnər] 20, 39
- ☐ **corruption** 名
  [kərápʃən] 56
- ☐ **cough** 動
  [kɔ́ːf] 35
- ☐ **counseling** 名
  [káunsəliŋ] 65
- ☐ **cover** 動
  [kávər] 107
- ☐ **cram** school 熟
  [krǽm] 6, 12
- ☐ **crash** through ~ 熟
  [krǽʃ] 72, 123
- ☐ **credit** 名
  [krédit] 50
- ☐ **cry** 動
  [krái] 61
- ☐ **curl** 動
  [kɔ́ːrl] 20
- ☐ **curly hair** 熟
  [héər] 26
- ☐ **customize** 動
  [kástəmàiz] 52

159

D

- [ ] **daily** 形
  [déili] 66
- [ ] **dark** 形
  [dáːrk] 67
- [ ] **dark glasses** 熟
  [glǽsiz] 42
- [ ] **dash** 動
  [dǽʃ] 28, 35
- [ ] **decide** 動
  [disáid] 48
- [ ] **decide to V** 熟
  [disáid] 11, 50, 64, 85, 97, 99, 104, 107, 117
- [ ] **defuse** 動
  [diːfjúːz] 27
- [ ] **~ degrees Centigrade** 熟
  [séntəgrèid] 16
- [ ] **delinquent** 名
  [dilíŋkwənt] 47, 52, 89
- [ ] **despite ~** 前
  [dispáit] 20
- [ ] **destination** 名
  [dèstənéiʃən] 82
- [ ] **devote A to B** 熟
  [divóut] 13
- [ ] **different** 形
  [dífərənt] 48
- [ ] **diligently** 副
  [dílədʒəntli] 47
- [ ] **dining hall** 熟
  [hɔ́ːl] 69
- [ ] **dinner** 名
  [dínər] 120
- [ ] **dizzy** 形
  [dízi] 16
- [ ] **doctor** 名
  [dáktər] 8
- [ ] **dodge** 動
  [dádʒ] 35
- [ ] **dogi** 名
  42
- [ ] **dojo** 名
  47
- [ ] **do well in school** 熟
  [wél] 26
- [ ] **downstairs** 名
  [dáunstéərz] 60
- [ ] **dozens of ~** 熟
  [dáznz] 6
- [ ] **dramatically** 副
  [drəmǽtikəli] 7
- [ ] **dream of ~** 熟
  [dríːm] 96
- [ ] **drip** 動
  [dríp] 72
- [ ] **driver** 名
  [dráivər] 75
- [ ] **driving school** 熟
  [dráiviŋ] 50
- [ ] **during ~** 前
  [djúəriŋ] 75

E

- [ ] **each other** 熟
  [íːtʃ] 34, 93
- [ ] **earn** 動
  [ə́ːrn] 93, 97
- [ ] **easily** 副
  [íːzili] 35, 50
- [ ] **easy-to-understand** 形
  [íːzi] 51
- [ ] **education industry** 熟
  [índəstri] 117
- [ ] **effort** 名
  [éfərt] 19, 127
- [ ] **either** 副
  [íːðər] 48
- [ ] **elementary school** 熟
  [èləméntəri] 11, 12, 24, 106
- [ ] **elite** 名
  [ilíːt] 8, 12
- [ ] **else** 副
  [éls] 88
- [ ] **employment exam** 熟
  [implɔ́imənt] 118
- [ ] **enemy** 名
  [énəmi] 56
- [ ] **engine** 名
  [éndʒin] 46, 80
- [ ] **English** 名
  [íŋgliʃ] 114
- [ ] **enjoy Ving** 熟
  [indʒɔ́i] 124
- [ ] **enough** 形
  [inʌ́f] 58, 97, 100
- [ ] **enough for ~ to V** 熟
  [inʌ́f] 50
- [ ] **enter** 動
  [éntər] 8, 24, 48, 65, 84, 92, 107, 116
- [ ] **entrance ceremony** 熟
  [sérəmòuni] 24, 26
- [ ] **entrance exam** 熟
  [éntrəns] 6, 12, 106

160

- □ **entrance** examination 熟
  [éntrəns] 24, 51, 106, 108
- □ **escape** 動
  [iskéip] 65
- □ **especially** 副
  [ispéʃəli] 82, 124
- □ **even** 副
  [íːvən] 8, 17, 32, 98, 107, 114, 126
- □ **even if** ..... 熟
  [if] 7, 127
- □ **even though** ..... 熟
  [ðóu] 88
- □ **every** day 熟
  [évri] 88
- □ **everyone** 代
  [évriwʌ̀n] 124
- □ **evidence** 名
  [évədəns] 61
- □ **exam** 名
  [igzǽm] 114
- □ **examination** 名
  [igzæ̀mənéiʃən] 13, 21, 50, 104, 114, 116
- □ **example** 名
  [igzǽmpl] 51
- □ **exceptional** 形
  [iksépʃənl] 58
- □ **excitement** 名
  [iksáitmənt] 30
- □ **Excuse** us. 熟
  [ikskjúːz] 90
- □ **existence** 名
  [igzístəns] 53
- □ **expect** 動
  [ikspékt] 14, 115
- □ **experience** 動
  [ikspíəriəns] 58
- □ **explain** 動
  [ikspléin] 24, 75
- □ **expression** 名
  [ikspréʃən] 104
- □ **eye** 名
  [ái] 61, 67, 89

F

- □ **face** 名
  [féis] 65, 68, 75
- □ **facedown** 副
  [féisdáun] 35
- □ **fail** 動
  [féil] 17, 24
- □ **failure** 名
  [féiljər] 16
- □ **fall** 動
  [fɔ́ːl] 36
- □ **fall** asleep 熟
  [fɔ́ːl] 123
- □ **fall** down 熟
  [fɔ́ːl] 28
- □ **farewell** 名
  [fɛ̀ərwél] 72
- □ **fashion model** 名
  [mάdl] 92
- □ **fear** 名
  [fíər] 90
- □ **feel** 動
  [fíːl] 30, 66, 104
- □ **feel** C 熟
  [fíːl] 16, 20
- □ feel **honored** 熟
  [άːnərd] 58
- □ **feeling** 名
  [fíːliŋ] 99
- □ **feel** like ..... 熟
  [fíːl] 121
- □ **fiction** 名
  [fíkʃən] 6
- □ **fight** 動名
  [fáit] 34, 41, 47, 48, 68
- □ **fighter** 名
  [fáitər] 41, 47
- □ **fighting** 名
  [fáitiŋ] 69, 105
- □ **finally** 副
  [fáinəli] 13, 19, 28, 69, 85, 99, 114
- □ **find** 動
  [fáind] 14, 94
- □ **finish** 動
  [fíniʃ] 69
- □ **firm** 形
  [fə́ːrm] 34
- □ **first choice** 名
  [tʃɔ́is] 114
- □ **first** year student 熟
  [fə́ːrst] 27
- □ **fist** 名
  [físt] 28, 35, 38
- □ **flinch** 動
  [flíntʃ] 56
- □ **float** 動
  [flóut] 121
- □ **floor** 名
  [flɔ́ːr] 36
- □ **fly** through the air 熟
  [flái] 38

161

☐ **follow** 動
[fálou] 7, 75

☐ **fool** 名
[fúːl] 127

☐ for a **long** time 熟
[lɔ́ːŋ] 120

☐ for a **moment** 熟
[móumənt] 19, 38

☐ for a **while** 熟
[hwáil] 39, 123

☐ **forehead** 名
[fɔ́ːrid] 41

☐ **forget** 動
[fərgét] 81

☐ **form** 名
[fɔ́ːrm] 34

☐ **former** 形
[fɔ́ːrmər] 98

☐ for **oneself** 熟
[wʌnsélf] 30

☐ **forward** 副
[fɔ́ːrwərd] 35, 73

☐ **freeze** 動
[fríːz] 28

☐ **funeral** 名
[fjúːnərəl] 76

☐ **funny** 形
[fʌ́ni] 34

☐ **futon** 名
[fjúːtɑn] 65

☐ **future** 名
[fjúːtʃər] 96

G

☐ **game** of cards 熟
[géim] 21

☐ **gang** 名
[gǽŋ] 56, 81, 85

☐ gang **leader** 熟
[líːdər] 53, 80

☐ gang **member** 熟
[mémbər] 80

☐ **gasoline** 名
[gǽsəlìːn] 72

☐ **gate** 名
[géit] 27

☐ **gather** 動
[gǽðər] 81

☐ **genius** 名
[dʒíːnjəs] 13

☐ **get** 動
[gét] 77, 118, 120

☐ get a **call** 熟
[kɔ́ːl] 108

☐ get a **cold** 熟
[kóuld] 16

☐ get **along** 熟
[əlɔ́ːŋ] 60

☐ get ~ **back** 熟
[bǽk] 97

☐ get **back** to ~ 熟
[bǽk] 41, 88, 94

☐ **get** C 熟
[gét] 33, 52

☐ get **home** 熟
[hóum] 17, 20

☐ get into **trouble** 熟
[trʌ́bl] 26

☐ **get** out of ~ 熟
[gét] 72

☐ **get** to ~ 熟
[gét] 121

☐ **get** ~ up 熟
[gét] 39

☐ **get** up 熟
[gét] 66

☐ **get** Ving 熟
[gét] 41

☐ **get** ~ Vpp 熟
[gét] 53

☐ **give** up ~ 熟
[gív] 7, 16, 66, 127

☐ **gladly** 副
[glǽdli] 58, 98

☐ **glare** at ~ 熟
[gléər] 65, 89

☐ **goal** 名
[góul] 8, 85

☐ go **along** with ~ 熟
[əlɔ́ːŋ] 59

☐ go **away** 熟
[əwéi] 39

☐ **gone** 形
[gɔ́ːn] 41, 94

☐ **go** on 熟
[góu] 85

☐ **go** on to ~ 熟
[góu] 48

☐ **go** out 熟
[góu] 65, 67

☐ **go** out of ~ 熟
[góu] 32, 42

☐ **go** out (with) ~ 熟
[góu] 92, 100

162

- ☐ **go** up to ~ 熟
  [góu]   21
- ☐ **go well** 熟
  [wél]   126
- ☐ **grab** 動
  [grǽb]   73, 76
- ☐ **grade** 名
  [gréid]   12, 42
- ☐ **graduate** 動
  [grǽdʒuèit]   88
- ☐ **graduate** from ~ 熟
  [grǽdʒuèit]   92
- ☐ **graduation** 名
  [grǽdʒuéiʃən]   117
- ☐ **graduation** ceremony 熟
  [grǽdʒuéiʃən]   88
- ☐ **greatest** 形
  [gréitist]   80
- ☐ **groan** 動
  [gróun]   67
- ☐ **guard** 名
  [gá:rd]   68
- ☐ **guardrail** 名
  [gá:rdrèil]   72, 123
- ☐ **guess** 名
  [gés]   115
- ☐ **gut** 名
  [gʌ́t]   58
- ☐ **guy** 名
  [gái]   7, 39, 41, 46, 56, 59, 89, 127

H

- ☐ **hair** 名
  [héər]   89
- ☐ **hand** 名
  [hǽnd]   73
- ☐ **hand** in ~ 熟
  [hǽnd]   105
- ☐ **hang** out with ~ 熟
  [hǽŋ]   25
- ☐ **hang** up ~ 熟
  [hǽŋ]   101
- ☐ **happen** 動
  [hǽpən]   75, 121, 126
- ☐ **harbor** 名
  [há:rbər]   54
- ☐ **hard** 副
  [há:rd]   36, 67
- ☐ **hate** 動
  [héit]   32
- ☐ **hate** Ving 熟
  [héit]   24

- ☐ **have** no **choice** but to V 熟
  [tʃɔ́is]   27
- ☐ **have** no **problem** Ving 熟
  [prábləm]   88
- ☐ **have** O V 熟
  [həv]   11
- ☐ **have** to V 熟
  [həv]   24, 60, 107
- ☐ **head** for ~ 熟
  [héd]   81, 82, 120
- ☐ **hear** 動
  [híər]   25, 34, 58, 60, 67, 90, 105
- ☐ **help** ~ out 熟
  [hélp]   27
- ☐ **help** O V 熟
  [hélp]   39
- ☐ **hierarchy** 名
  [háiərà:rki]   53
- ☐ **highest** 形
  [háiist]   118
- ☐ **high** school 熟
  [hái]   34, 88
- ☐ **history** 名
  [hístəri]   118
- ☐ **hit** 動
  [hít]   75
- ☐ **hold** 動
  [hóuld]   75, 108
- ☐ **honor** 名
  [ánər]   80
- ☐ **hop** in 熟
  [háp]   46
- ☐ **how** 副
  [háu]   104
- ☐ **how** ..... 副
  [háu]   116
- ☐ **how** about ~ ? 熟
  [háu]   21
- ☐ **however** 副
  [hauévər]   20, 107
- ☐ **how** to V 熟
  [háu]   51, 107
- ☐ **huge** 形
  [hjú:dʒ]   72, 80, 108
- ☐ **hundred** 名
  [hʌ́ndrəd]   118

I

- ☐ ID **number** 熟
  [nʌ́mbər]   14
- ☐ **if** ..... 接
  [if]   36, 88, 127

163

☐ **ignore** 動
[ignɔ́:r] 32

☐ **imagine** 動
[imǽdʒin] 59

☐ **immediately** 副
[imí:diətli] 84, 109

☐ **impress** 動
[imprés] 51

☐ **improve** 動
[imprú:v] 7

☐ **impulsive** 形
[impʌ́lsiv] 26

☐ in a **daze** 熟
[déiz] 38

☐ in **addition** to ~ 熟
[ədíʃən] 50

☐ in a **row** 熟
[róu] 54

☐ **individual** 形
[ìndəvídʒuəl] 53

☐ **information** 名
[ìnfərméiʃən] 51

☐ in **front** 熟
[frʌ́nt] 67, 80, 82

☐ in **front** of ~ 熟
[frʌ́nt] 42, 56, 73, 84, 121

☐ in less than a **minute** 熟
[mínit] 68

☐ in **order** to V 熟
[ɔ́:rdər] 84

☐ **inspire** 動
[inspáiər] 6

☐ **inspiring** 形
[inspáiəriŋ] 7

☐ **instantly** 副
[ínstəntli] 75

☐ **instead** 副
[instéd] 34, 105

☐ **instead** of ~ 熟
[instéd] 97

☐ **instinctively** 副
[instíŋktivli] 19

☐ **institution** 名
[ìnstətjú:ʃən] 65, 69

☐ **intelligence** 名
[intélədʒəns] 20

☐ **intend** to V 熟
[inténd] 109

☐ **interesting** 形
[íntərəstiŋ] 33

☐ **interference** 名
[ìntərfíərəns] 82

☐ **intersection** 名
[ìntərsékʃən] 72

☐ it is **natural** that ..... 熟
[nǽtʃərəl] 11

☐ It **seems** that ..... 熟
[sí:mz] 58

J

☐ **jacket** 名
[dʒǽkit] 56

☐ **January** 名
[dʒǽnjuèri] 108

☐ **Japanese** 名
[dʒæpəní:z] 106, 115, 116

☐ Japanese **classics** 名
[klǽsiks] 114

☐ Japanese **history** 名
[hístəri] 106, 115, 116

☐ Japanese **literature** 名
[lítərətʃər] 6, 114, 116

☐ **join** 動
[dʒɔ́in] 42, 82, 108

☐ **juku** 名
[dʒúku] 6

☐ **junior** high 熟
[dʒú:njər] 48, 107

☐ **junior** high school 熟
[dʒú:njər] 12, 34, 42, 51, 104, 106

☐ **just** 副
[dʒʌ́st] 16, 19

☐ **just** ..... 熟
[dʒʌ́st] 21, 30, 32, 59, 61, 77, 90

☐ **juvenile corrective** institution 熟
[kəréktiv] 64

☐ **juvenile** delinquency 熟
[dʒú:vənl] 53

☐ **juvenile** delinquent 熟
[dʒú:vənl] 48

K

☐ **karate** 名
[kərá:ti] 41

☐ **Karate** dojo 熟
[kərá:ti] 33

☐ **kata** 名
34

☐ **keep** to ~ 熟
[kí:p] 8, 56

☐ **keep** up with ~ 熟
[kí:p] 13

☐ **keep** Ving 熟
[kí:p] 88

164

- □ **kid** 名
  [kíd] 10
- □ **kill** 動
  [kíl] 36
- □ **kindergarten** 名
  [kíndərgɑ̀ːrtn] 11
- □ **knife** 名
  [náif] 109
- □ **knock** ~ down 熟
  [nák] 67
- □ **knock** out ~ 熟
  [nák] 35, 38
- □ **know** 動
  [nóu] 89, 96
- □ **knowledge** 名
  [nálidʒ] 106

L

- □ **land** 動
  [lǽnd] 35, 38
- □ **last** 動形
  [lǽst] 11, 19, 80
- □ **later** 副
  [léitər] 30
- □ **laugh** 動
  [lǽf] 34
- □ **law** 名
  [lɔ́ː] 59, 101
- □ **lawyer** 名
  [lɔ́ːjər] 8, 101
- □ **lead** 動
  [líːd] 64
- □ **lead** ~ out 熟
  [líːd] 70
- □ **lead** up 熟
  [líːd] 121
- □ **lean** 動
  [líːn] 35
- □ **lean** back 熟
  [líːn] 28
- □ **learn** 動
  [lə́ːrn] 99, 123
- □ **leave** 動
  [líːv] 26, 68, 69, 82, 90, 97, 124
- □ **leave** ~ **behind** 熟
  [biháind] 11
- □ **lecture** 名
  [léktʃər] 50
- □ **less** and less 熟
  [lés] 93
- □ **let** O V 熟
  [lét] 84
- □ **license** 名
  [láisəns] 98
- □ **lie** 動
  [lái] 65, 67, 73, 76
- □ **life** 名
  [láif] 8, 96, 124
- □ **life insurance** 名
  [inʃúərəns] 10
- □ **light** 名
  [láit] 75
- □ **like** ~ 動
  [láik] 33, 34, 42, 48, 68, 88, 93, 101, 107, 114, 117, 126
- □ **line** up 熟
  [láin] 54
- □ **list** 名
  [líst] 14
- □ **live** 動
  [lív] 92, 124
- □ **local** 形
  [lóukəl] 76
- □ **locker room** 名
  [rúːm] 42
- □ **look** 名動
  [lúk] 20, 75
- □ **look at** ~ 熟
  [lúk] 39, 42, 56, 92
- □ **look** back 熟
  [lúk] 121
- □ **look** C 熟
  [lúk] 33, 69
- □ **look for** ~ 熟
  [lúk] 14, 96
- □ **look forward** to Ving 熟
  [fɔ́ːrwərd] 93
- □ **look into** ~ 熟
  [lúk] 90
- □ **look like** ~ 熟
  [lúk] 27, 34
- □ **look of anger** 熟
  [lúk] 41
- □ **look** ~ **up** 熟
  [lúk] 97, 99
- □ **lose** 動
  [lúːz] 75
- □ **loud** 動
  [láud] 34, 38, 52
- □ **loudly** 副
  [láudli] 46
- □ **loudspeaker** 名
  [láudspìːkər] 84
- □ **love** 動
  [lʌ́v] 96

- ☐ **luck** 名
  [lʌ́k] ... 19

M

- ☐ make an **effort** 熟
  [éfərt] ... 13
- ☐ make an **excuse** 熟
  [ikskjúːs] ... 17
- ☐ **make** O C 熟
  [méik] ... 52
- ☐ **make** O V 熟
  [méik] ... 16, 104
- ☐ **manager** 名
  [mǽnidʒər] ... 8
- ☐ **mangle** 動
  [mǽŋgl] ... 72
- ☐ **many** 形
  [méni] ... 8, 25
- ☐ **mark** 名
  [máːrk] ... 68
- ☐ **meal** 名
  [míːl] ... 93
- ☐ **mean** 動
  [míːn] ... 58, 107
- ☐ **media** 名
  [míːdiə] ... 76
- ☐ **meet** 動
  [míːt] ... 60, 100
- ☐ **member** 名
  [mémbər] ... 8
- ☐ **memorize** 動
  [méməràiz] ... 51
- ☐ **memory** 名
  [méməri] ... 50
- ☐ **method** 名
  [méθəd] ... 7
- ☐ **midnight** 名
  [mídnàit] ... 54
- ☐ **might** have Vpp 熟
  [máit] ... 19
- ☐ **might** V 熟
  [máit] ... 126
- ☐ **minimum** 形
  [mínəməm] ... 13
- ☐ **miserable** 形
  [mízərəbl] ... 20, 25
- ☐ **mission** 名
  [míʃən] ... 114
- ☐ **mistake** 名
  [mistéik] ... 126
- ☐ **model** 名
  [mádl] ... 100

- ☐ **moment** 名
  [móumənt] ... 126
- ☐ **month** 名
  [mʌ́nθ] ... 98
- ☐ monthly **salary** 熟
  [sǽləri] ... 98
- ☐ **more** 形
  [mɔ́ːr] ... 25, 84
- ☐ **most** of ~ 熟
  [móust] ... 115
- ☐ **motivate** 動
  [móutəvèit] ... 7, 116
- ☐ **motivation** 名
  [mòutəvéiʃən] ... 24
- ☐ **motorcycle** gang 熟
  [móutərsàikl] ... 46, 81, 98
- ☐ motorcycle **license** 熟
  [láisəns] ... 50
- ☐ **much** 副形
  [mʌ́tʃ] ... 26, 38, 50, 76
- ☐ **much** more 熟
  [mʌ́tʃ] ... 97
- ☐ **muffler** 名
  [mʌ́flər] ... 52
- ☐ municipal **government** 熟
  [gʌ́vərnmənt] ... 108

N

- ☐ **name** 動
  [néim] ... 54, 81, 100
- ☐ **name** O C 熟
  [néim] ... 10
- ☐ **naturally** 副
  [nǽtʃərəli] ... 52
- ☐ **neighboring** 形
  [néibəriŋ] ... 82
- ☐ **never** 副
  [névər] ... 60, 127
- ☐ **never** ..... 副
  [névər] ... 30
- ☐ New Year's **Eve** 熟
  [íːv] ... 82
- ☐ **Nice** to meet you. 熟
  [náis] ... 89
- ☐ **night** 名
  [náit] ... 114
- ☐ **nod** 動
  [nád] ... 19, 39, 41
- ☐ **normal** life 熟
  [nɔ́ːrməl] ... 88
- ☐ **not** ..... at all 熟
  [nát] ... 24, 32, 47

- [ ] **note** 名
 [nóut] 94, 96
- [ ] **notice** 動
 [nóutis] 33, 52, 97
- [ ] not **move** an inch 熟
 [mú:v] 66
- [ ] not **only** A but also B 熟
 [óunli] 118
- [ ] **November** 名
 [nouvémbər] 80
- [ ] **number** 名
 [nʌ́mbər] 99
- [ ] **numerous** 形
 [njú:mərəs] 47, 48
- [ ] **nurture** 動
 [nə́:rtʃər] 8

O

- [ ] **o' clock** 副
 [əklák] 85
- [ ] **observe** 動
 [əbzə́:rv] 53, 97
- [ ] of **course** 熟
 [kɔ́:rs] 16, 32
- [ ] **offer** 名動
 [ɔ́:fər] 58, 120
- [ ] **officer** 名
 [ɔ́:fisər] 70
- [ ] **old** 形
 [óuld] 25
- [ ] **one** by one 熟
 [wʌ́n] 69
- [ ] **one** day 熟
 [wʌ́n] 94
- [ ] on the **day** before ~ 熟
 [déi] 108
- [ ] on the **day** of ~ 熟
 [déi] 17, 21, 88, 104
- [ ] on the **edge** of ~ 熟
 [édʒ] 54, 56
- [ ] **on** Ving 熟
 [ən] 34
- [ ] **opponent** 名
 [əpóunənt] 35, 68
- [ ] **order** 人 to V 熟
 [ɔ́:rdər] 80
- [ ] **organized** 形
 [ɔ́:rgənàizd] 53
- [ ] **ornament** 名
 [ɔ́:rnəmənt] 52
- [ ] **other** 形
 [ʌ́ðər] 10, 59, 65

- [ ] **others** 代
 [ʌ́ðərz] 85
- [ ] **out** of ~ 熟
 [áut] 64
- [ ] **over** 副
 [óuvər] 76
- [ ] **over** ~ 前
 [óuvər] 16, 58, 65, 105, 107, 115, 126
- [ ] **overall** 副
 [óuvərɔ́:l] 76, 80
- [ ] **overcome** 動
 [òuvərkʌ́m] 127
- [ ] **own** 形動
 [óun] 6, 93
- [ ] **owner** 名
 [óunər] 99, 117

P

- [ ] pachinko **parlor** 熟
 [pá:rlər] 93
- [ ] **pack** 動
 [pǽk] 69
- [ ] **pale** 形
 [péil] 90
- [ ] **pant** 動
 [pǽnt] 36
- [ ] **park** 動
 [pá:rk] 42
- [ ] **parking** lot 熟
 [pá:rkiŋ] 80, 85
- [ ] **part** 名
 [pá:rt] 106, 109
- [ ] **part**-time 熟
 [pá:rt] 92, 100
- [ ] **pass** 動
 [pǽs] 7, 11, 13, 19, 33, 47, 50, 69, 114, 115, 116, 118
- [ ] **passenger** seat 熟
 [pǽsəndʒər] 70, 120
- [ ] **pass** out 熟
 [pǽs] 28
- [ ] pass the **examination** 熟
 [igzæmənéiʃən] 120
- [ ] **patrol** car 熟
 [pətróul] 64, 72, 84
- [ ] **pay** 動
 [péi] 99
- [ ] **pay** off 熟
 [péi] 19
- [ ] **perhaps** 副
 [pərhǽps] 27
- [ ] **permed** 形
 [pə:rmd] 56

- ☐ **person** 名
  [pə́ːrsn] 96
- ☐ **personality** 名
  [pə̀ːrsənǽləti] 26
- ☐ **phone** 名
  [fóun] 101
- ☐ **pick** ~ up 熟
  [pík] 46
- ☐ **pillow** 名
  [pílou] 39, 65
- ☐ **pin** ~ down 熟
  [pín] 65
- ☐ **plan** to V 熟
  [plǽn] 13, 109
- ☐ **play** 動
  [pléi] 46
- ☐ **play** cards 熟
  [pléi] 59
- ☐ **police** car 熟
  [pəlíːs] 84
- ☐ **police** officer 熟
  [pəlíːs] 64, 72
- ☐ **police** patrol car 熟
  [pəlíːs] 70, 84
- ☐ **police** station 熟
  [pəlíːs] 61, 64
- ☐ **popular** 形
  [pάpjulər] 7, 116
- ☐ **position** 名
  [pəzíʃən] 58
- ☐ **post** 動
  [póust] 14
- ☐ **pound** 動
  [páund] 27, 92
- ☐ **pour** 動
  [pɔ́ːr] 28
- ☐ **power** 動名
  [páuər] 41, 116
- ☐ **practice** 名
  [prǽktis] 33, 42
- ☐ **practice** exam 熟
  [prǽktis] 107
- ☐ **praise** 動
  [préiz] 11
- ☐ **prefecture** 名
  [príːfektʃər] 84
- ☐ **prepared** 形
  [pripéərd] 67
- ☐ **prepare** for ~ 熟
  [pripéər] 6, 50, 93, 109
- ☐ **prep** school 熟
  [prép] 6, 117
- ☐ **prestigious** 形
  [prestídʒiəs] 6, 11, 12, 89, 105, 106
- ☐ **pretty** well 熟
  [príti] 106
- ☐ **privately** 副
  [práivətli] 6
- ☐ **private** school 熟
  [práivət] 48
- ☐ **problem** 名
  [prάbləm] 99
- ☐ **prodigy** 名
  [prάdədʒi] 10
- ☐ **promise** to V 熟
  [prάmis] 99
- ☐ **public** junior high school 熟
  [pʌ́blik] 24
- ☐ **public** school 熟
  [pʌ́blik] 12, 20
- ☐ **punch** 動
  [pʌ́ntʃ] 36, 38, 67
- ☐ **put** in ~ 熟
  [pút] 127
- ☐ **put** up ~ 熟
  [pút] 14

Q

- ☐ **question** 名
  [kwéstʃən] 60
- ☐ **questioning** 名
  [kwéstʃəniŋ] 64
- ☐ **quit** 動
  [kwít] 81, 85
- ☐ **quite** 副
  [kwáit] 53, 68, 115
- ☐ **quite** a lot of ~ 熟
  [kwáit] 98
- ☐ **quit** Ving 熟
  [kwít] 107

R

- ☐ **race** toward ~ 熟
  [réis] 54
- ☐ **racing** circuit 熟
  [réisiŋ] 81
- ☐ **raise** 動
  [réiz] 38
- ☐ **reach** 動
  [ríːtʃ] 82, 85
- ☐ **reach** ~ out 熟
  [ríːtʃ] 123
- ☐ **reactivate** 動
  [riǽktəvèit] 106

- ☐ **real** 形
  [ríːəl] 121
- ☐ **realize** 動
  [ríːəlàiz] 26
- ☐ **really** 副
  [ríːəli] 109
- ☐ **reason** 名
  [ríːzn] 105
- ☐ **recall** 動
  [rikɔ́ːl] 106
- ☐ **recognize** 動
  [rékəgnàiz] 53
- ☐ **record** 名
  [rékərd] 105
- ☐ **relate** to ~ 熟
  [riléit] 52
- ☐ **related** to ~ 熟
  [riléitid] 52
- ☐ **relieve** 動
  [rilíːv] 109
- ☐ **remember** 動
  [rimémbər] 96, 104, 126
- ☐ **remove** 動
  [rimúːv] 52
- ☐ **reporter** 名
  [ripɔ́ːrtər] 76
- ☐ **required** 形
  [rikwáiərd] 107
- ☐ **resignation** 名
  [rèzignéiʃən] 105
- ☐ **respect** 名
  [rispékt] 81
- ☐ **respected** 形
  [rispéktid] 58
- ☐ **respond** to ~ 熟
  [rispánd] 19
- ☐ **rest** 動
  [rést] 114
- ☐ **result** 名
  [rizʌ́lt] 21, 120
- ☐ **ride** 名
  [ráid] 120
- ☐ **right** 名
  [ráit] 73
- ☐ **rival** 名
  [ráivəl] 12
- ☐ **roar** 動
  [rɔ́ːr] 46, 80
- ☐ **rock'n'roll** music 熟
  [rὰkənróul] 46
- ☐ **role** 名
  [róul] 53
- ☐ **roll** 動
  [róul] 36
- ☐ **roll** down ~ 熟
  [róul] 75, 123
- ☐ **roll** over 熟
  [róul] 123
- ☐ **rubber** 名
  [rʌ́bər] 72
- ☐ **ruin** 動
  [rúːin] 110
- ☐ **run** 名
  [rʌ́n] 80
- ☐ **run** around 熟
  [rʌ́n] 72
- ☐ **run** into ~ 熟
  [rʌ́n] 69

S

- ☐ **sacrifice** 動
  [sǽkrəfàis] 84
- ☐ **sad** 形
  [sǽd] 25
- ☐ **salesman** 名
  [séilzmən] 92, 99
- ☐ **salespeople** 名
  [séilzpìːpl] 97
- ☐ **salesperson** 名
  [séilzpɜ̀ːrsn] 97, 98
- ☐ **same** 形
  [séim] 32
- ☐ **save** 動
  [séiv] 90, 117
- ☐ **say** 動
  [séi] 21
- ☐ **say goodbye** to ~ 熟
  [gùdbái] 64
- ☐ **school gang** leader 熟
  [gǽŋ] 30
- ☐ **school uniform** 熟
  [júːnəfɔ̀ːrm] 73
- ☐ **scold** 動
  [skóuld] 32
- ☐ **score** 名
  [skɔ́ːr] 7, 13, 107, 118
- ☐ **scream** 動
  [skríːm] 115
- ☐ **screech** 動
  [skríːtʃ] 56
- ☐ **sedan** 名
  [sidǽn] 42, 54, 56
- ☐ **seem** to be C 熟
  [síːm] 73

169

- [ ] **seem** to V 㒹
 [síːm] 25
- [ ] **send** 動
 [sénd] 64
- [ ] **sentence** 名
 [séntəns] 69
- [ ] **serious** 形
 [síəriəs] 54, 69
- [ ] **several** 形
 [sévərəl] 33, 58, 76, 118
- [ ] **sex** 名
 [séks] 60
- [ ] **share** 動
 [ʃéər] 65
- [ ] **sharp** pain 㒹
 [ʃɑːrp] 66
- [ ] **shine** 動
 [ʃáin] 80
- [ ] **short**-tempered 形
 [ʃɔːrt] 26
- [ ] **show** 動
 [ʃóu] 81, 90
- [ ] **single** 形
 [síŋgl] 114
- [ ] **siren** 名
 [sáiərən] 70
- [ ] **sit** 動
 [sít] 70, 85
- [ ] **sit** a test 㒹
 [sít] 17
- [ ] **situation** 名
 [sìtʃuéiʃən] 27
- [ ] **skill** 名
 [skíl] 51, 69
- [ ] **skyrocket** 動
 [skáirɑ̀kit] 98
- [ ] **slightly** 副
 [sláitli] 20
- [ ] **slow** down 㒹
 [slóu] 84
- [ ] **slowly** 副
 [slóuli] 121
- [ ] **smart** 形
 [smɑːrt] 10, 101
- [ ] **smell** 動
 [smél] 72
- [ ] **smile** 動
 [smáil] 21
- [ ] **smile** at ~ 㒹
 [smáil] 123
- [ ] **smile** back 㒹
 [smáil] 21
- [ ] **smoke** a **cigarette** 㒹
 [sigərét] 32
- [ ] **sneer** at ~ 㒹
 [sníər] 66
- [ ] **so** 接副
 [sóu] 7, 17, 21, 25, 47, 48, 51, 61, 88, 96, 99, 100, 105, 117, 120, 127
- [ ] **sob** 動
 [sɑ́b] 28
- [ ] **society** 名
 [səsáiəti] 59, 105, 126
- [ ] **solve** 動
 [sɑ́lv] 51, 99
- [ ] **some** 代形
 [sʌ́m] 54, 60, 89, 90
- [ ] **somebody** else 㒹
 [sʌ́mbɑ̀di] 100
- [ ] **something** 代
 [sʌ́mθiŋ] 104
- [ ] **something** else 㒹
 [sʌ́mθiŋ] 100
- [ ] **sometimes** 副
 [sʌ́mtàimz] 32, 126
- [ ] **soon** 副
 [súːn] 116
- [ ] **sorry** 形
 [sɑ́ri] 19, 25, 96, 101
- [ ] **sorry** to V 㒹
 [sɑ́ri] 99
- [ ] **so** ~ that S V 㒹
 [sóu] 34
- [ ] **so** that S will V 㒹
 [sóu] 52
- [ ] **soul** 名
 [sóul] 81
- [ ] **spare** 形
 [spéər] 42
- [ ] **spark** 動
 [spɑ́ːrk] 104
- [ ] **special** 形
 [spéʃəl] 98, 100
- [ ] **speed** 動
 [spíːd] 56
- [ ] **spend** 動
 [spénd] 64, 76
- [ ] **spend** 時間 Ving 㒹
 [spénd] 48
- [ ] **square** 名
 [skwéər] 28
- [ ] **squat** down 㒹
 [skwɑ́t] 73
- [ ] **stagger** 動
 [stǽgər] 38

- ☐ **stairs** 名
  [stéərz] 61, 120, 123
- ☐ **stand** 動
  [sténd] 73
- ☐ **stand** up 熟
  [sténd] 109
- ☐ **stare** at ~ 熟
  [stéər] 76
- ☐ **start** off 熟
  [stá:rt] 70
- ☐ **start** to V 熟
  [stá:rt] 8, 42, 121
- ☐ **start** Ving 熟
  [stá:rt] 27, 92
- ☐ **station** 名
  [stéiʃən] 89
- ☐ **stomach** 名
  [stʌ́mək] 36, 67
- ☐ **story** 名
  [stɔ́:ri] 32
- ☐ **stout** 形
  [stáut] 56
- ☐ **straight** 形
  [stréit] 89
- ☐ **strangely** 副
  [stréindʒli] 82
- ☐ **strategy** 名
  [strǽtədʒi] 106
- ☐ **strength** 名
  [stréŋkθ] 30
- ☐ **stress** 名
  [strés] 109
- ☐ **stretcher** 名
  [strétʃər] 73
- ☐ **strict** 形
  [stríkt] 53
- ☐ **strictly** 副
  [stríktli] 53
- ☐ **struggle** 動
  [strʌ́gl] 117
- ☐ **stuff** 名
  [stʌ́f] 69, 94
- ☐ **subject** 名
  [sʌ́bdʒikt] 106, 108, 114
- ☐ **suburb** 名
  [sʌ́bə:rb] 10
- ☐ **sudden** 形
  [sʌ́dn] 72, 120
- ☐ **suddenly** 副
  [sʌ́dnli] 54, 60, 66, 76, 109
- ☐ **suit** 名
  [sú:t | sjú:t] 60, 109, 110

- ☐ **summon** 動
  [sʌ́mən] 53, 54
- ☐ **sunrise** 名
  [sʌ́nràiz] 85
- ☐ **surreal** 形
  [sərí:əl] 73
- ☐ **surround** 動
  [səráund] 27, 89
- ☐ **sympathetic** 形
  [sìmpəθétik] 20

T

- ☐ **table** 名
  [téibl] 94
- ☐ **take** 動
  [téik] 12, 16, 116
- ☐ take a **walk** 熟
  [wɔ́:k] 32
- ☐ **take** care of ~ 熟
  [téik] 39
- ☐ take it for **granted** that SV 熟
  [grǽntid] 11, 26
- ☐ take **medicine** 熟
  [médəsin] 16
- ☐ **take** 人 to ~ 熟
  [téik] 61, 65
- ☐ **take** the entrance exam 熟
  [téik] 11
- ☐ take **turns** 熟
  [tə́:rnz] 66
- ☐ **talk** 動
  [tɔ́:k] 85, 120
- ☐ **talk** about ~ 熟
  [tɔ́:k] 32
- ☐ **talk** to ~ 熟
  [tɔ́:k] 33
- ☐ **talk** with ~ 熟
  [tɔ́:k] 25
- ☐ teaching **skill** 熟
  [skíl] 117
- ☐ **tear** 名
  [tíər] 61, 75, 89
- ☐ **technique** 名
  [tekní:k] 51, 97
- ☐ **temperature** 名
  [témpərətʃər] 16
- ☐ **than** ~ 接
  [ðən] 10, 73
- ☐ **thankful** 形
  [θǽŋkfəl] 124, 126
- ☐ **thanks** to ~ 熟
  [θǽŋks] 52

171

- ☐ **thank** you for Ving 熟
  [θǽŋk]   46, 90
- ☐ the **best** of the best 熟
  [bést]   117
- ☐ the **day** before 熟
  [déi]   96
- ☐ the **first** time 熟
  [fə́:rst]   85, 92
- ☐ **theme** park 熟
  [θí:m]   80
- ☐ the **middle** of ~ 熟
  [mídl]   108
- ☐ the **next** day 熟
  [nékst]   17, 68
- ☐ the **only** ~ 熟
  [óunli]   110
- ☐ the **others** 熟
  [ʌ́ðərz]   84
- ☐ the **prime** of life 熟
  [práim]   59
- ☐ the **public** 熟
  [pʌ́blik]   53
- ☐ the **top** of ~ 熟
  [táp]   61, 124
- ☐ **think** 動
  [θíŋk]   30, 46, 127
- ☐ This is **how** ~ 熟
  [háu]   92
- ☐ this **time** 熟
  [táim]   36, 67
- ☐ **thousands** of ~ 熟
  [θáuzəndz]   82
- ☐ **threatening** 形
  [θrétniŋ]   27
- ☐ **through** ~ 前
  [θrú:]   17, 117
- ☐ **throughout** ~ 前
  [θru:áut]   47
- ☐ **throw** 動
  [θróu]   38
- ☐ **tidy** up ~ 熟
  [táidi]   11
- ☐ **tinted** 形
  [tíntid]   42
- ☐ **together** 副
  [təgéðər]   120
- ☐ **tone** 名
  [tóun]   27
- ☐ to tell the **truth** 熟
  [trú:θ]   25, 100
- ☐ **touch** 動
  [tʌ́tʃ]   25, 123

- ☐ **toward** ~ 前
  [tɔ́:rd]   28, 35, 36, 67, 68
- ☐ **towel** 名
  [táuəl]   39
- ☐ **tragedy** 名
  [trǽdʒədi]   81
- ☐ **training** 名
  [tréiniŋ]   50
- ☐ **treat** 動
  [trí:t]   104
- ☐ **tremble** with ~ 熟
  [trémbl]   90
- ☐ **trial** 名
  [tráiəl]   64
- ☐ **try** to V 熟
  [trái]   65, 105
- ☐ **tumble** 動
  [tʌ́mbl]   123
- ☐ **turn** 動
  [tə́:rn]   50, 90, 108
- ☐ **turn** out that ..... 熟
  [tə́:rn]   30
- ☐ **twice** 副
  [twáis]   93

U

- ☐ **unfair** 形
  [ʌnféər]   20, 126
- ☐ **unfairness** 名
  [ʌnféərnəs]   59, 105
- ☐ **uniform** 名
  [jú:nəfɔ̀:rm]   89
- ☐ **university** 名
  [jù:nəvə́:rsəti]   6, 101
- ☐ **unlike** ~ 前
  [ʌnláik]   12
- ☐ **unpopular** 形
  [ʌnpápjulər]   48
- ☐ **unsteady** 形
  [ʌnstédi]   38
- ☐ **until** ~ 前
  [əntíl]   108, 114
- ☐ **upstairs** 副
  [ʌ́pstéərz]   21
- ☐ **upwards** 副
  [ʌ́pwərdz]   20
- ☐ **used** car 熟
  [jú:zd]   92
- ☐ **used** to V 熟
  [jú:st]   52, 81, 82
- ☐ **usual** 形
  [jú:ʒuəl]   73

172

- ☐ **usually** 副
 [júːʒuəli] 82, 93
- ☐ **utilize** 動
 [júːtəlàiz] 97

V

- ☐ **valuable** 形
 [vǽljuəbl] 26
- ☐ **various** 形
 [vέəriəs] 52
- ☐ **very** much 熟
 [véri] 93
- ☐ **visitor** 名
 [vízitər] 60
- ☐ **voluntarily** 副
 [vɑ̀ləntέərəli] 11

W

- ☐ **waiting** 形
 [wéitiŋ] 64
- ☐ **walk** up to ~ 熟
 [wɔ́ːk] 89
- ☐ **want** to V 熟
 [wɑ́nt] 16, 24, 89, 100, 104, 114, 124
- ☐ **want** 人 to V 熟
 [wɑ́nt] 124
- ☐ **waste** 動
 [wéist] 108, 126
- ☐ **watch** 動
 [wɑ́tʃ] 61
- ☐ **waterfront** 名
 [wɔ́ːtərfrʌ̀nt] 54, 56
- ☐ **way** to ~ 熟
 [wéi] 90
- ☐ **weakling** 名
 [wíːkliŋ] 34
- ☐ **wear** 動
 [wέər] 89
- ☐ **welcome** 動
 [wélkəm] 21
- ☐ **well** 副
 [wél] 90, 100, 126
- ☐ **Well** done. 熟
 [wél] 58
- ☐ **wet** 形
 [wét] 39
- ☐ what is **called** 熟
 [kɔ́ːld] 12
- ☐ **what** ~ was 熟
 [hwɑ́t] 75
- ☐ **when** ..... 接
 [hwén] 13, 17, 20, 26, 33, 39, 41, 51, 66, 75, 84, 94, 105, 106, 121

- ☐ **whether** ..... 接
 [hwéðər] 25, 81, 96
- ☐ **while** ..... 接
 [hwáil] 93, 123
- ☐ **with** ~ 前
 [wíð] 41
- ☐ with all one's **might** 熟
 [máit] 35
- ☐ with **joy** 熟
 [dʒɔ́i] 115
- ☐ **without** Ving 熟
 [wiðáut] 16, 41
- ☐ **wonder** ..... 動
 [wʌ́ndər] 54
- ☐ **word** 名
 [wə́ːrd] 19, 41, 104, 107, 116
- ☐ **work** 名動
 [wə́ːrk] 6, 8, 10, 47
- ☐ **worker** 名
 [wə́ːrkər] 72
- ☐ **worried** 形
 [wə́ːrid] 96
- ☐ **worry** 動
 [wə́ːri] 19, 21, 99
- ☐ **worry** about ~ 熟
 [wə́ːri] 13
- ☐ **worthless** 形
 [wə́ːθlis] 104
- ☐ **worthy** of ~ 熟
 [wə́ːrði] 93
- ☐ **Would** you like to V ? 熟
 [wúd] 27
- ☐ **wrong** 形
 [rɔ́ːŋ] 59

Y

- ☐ **yen** 名
 [jén] 99, 100
- ☐ **younger** 形
 [jʌ́ŋgər] 10

173

MEMO

●大学受験 英文多読シリーズ
生きろ!

発行日：2013年11月4日　初版発行
　　　　2022年7月16日　第6版発行

著　者：安河内哲也
発行者：永瀬昭幸

編集担当：村本悠
発行所：株式会社ナガセ
　　　　〒180-0003　東京都武蔵野市吉祥寺南1-29-2
　　　　出版事業部(東進ブックス)
　　　　TEL：0422-70-7456 ／ FAX：0422-70-7457
　　　　URL：http://www.toshin.com/books/
　　　　(本書を含む東進ブックスの最新情報は上記「WEB書店」をご覧ください)

原案：吉野敬介
カバー・本文デザイン：LIGHTNING
イラスト：芹沢直樹
執筆協力・校閲：Matthew Radich ／ Mickey Acorn
翻訳・編集協力：山越友子

DTP：株式会社秀文社
印刷・製本：日経印刷株式会社
音声収録・編集：英語教育協議会(ELEC英語研修所)
音声出演：安河内哲也／ Rachel Walzer

※落丁・乱丁本は東進WEB書店のお問い合せよりお申し出ください。但し、古書店で本書を購入されている場合は、お取り替えできません。
※本書を無断で複写・複製・転載することを禁じます。

©Tetsuya Yasukochi 2013 Printed in Japan
ISBN978-4-89085-584-1　C7382

音声ダウンロードサイト

http://www.toshin.com/books/

※音声ダウンロードの際は、下記のパスワードが必要です。詳細は上記のサイトをご参照ください。

ID：eibuntadoku　Password：ikirodaiki

※この物語は、東進ハイスクール講師・吉野敬介氏の半生をもとにしたフィクションです。

東進ブックス

編集部より

この本を読み終えた君に オススメの3冊!

英文多読シリーズ第1弾!!
女子高生のリサは、死者の声が聴こえるという特殊能力の持ち主。リサを待ち受ける使命とは…!?

英文多読シリーズ第2弾!!
舞台は東京。親も家も失い、ある日突然ホームレスになったメグ。ある時、謎の男に出会って…!?

ミラクルアイドルメグ2巻!! いよいよ物語は後編クライマックスへ突入!! トップスターになれるのは一体誰…!?

体験授業

この本を書いた講師の授業を受けてみませんか?

東進では有名実力講師陣の授業を無料で体験できる『体験授業』を行っています。
「わかる」授業、「完璧に」理解できるシステム、そして最後まで「頑張れる」雰囲気を実際に体験してください。

※1講座 (90分×1回) を受講できます。
※お電話または東進ドットコムでご予約ください。
連絡先は付録9ページをご覧ください。
※お友達同士でも受講できます。

安河内先生の主な担当講座　※2022年度
「有名大突破!戦略英語解法」など

東進の合格の秘訣が次ページに

合格の秘訣1 全国屈指の実力講師陣

東進の実力講師陣
数多くのベストセラー参考書を執筆!!

東進ハイスクール・東進衛星予備校では、そうそうたる講師陣が君を熱く指導する!

本気で実力をつけたいと思うなら、やはり根本から理解させてくれる一流講師の授業を受けることが大切です。東進の講師は、日本全国から選りすぐられた大学受験のプロフェッショナル。何万人もの受験生を志望校合格へ導いてきたエキスパート達です。

英語

安河内 哲也 先生 [英語]
日本を代表する英語の伝道師。ベストセラーも多数。

今井 宏 先生 [英語] 
予備校界のカリスマ。抱腹絶倒の名講義を見逃すな。

渡辺 勝彦 先生 [英語]
「スーパー速読法」で難解な長文問題の速読即解を可能にする「予備校界の達人」!

宮崎 尊 先生 [英語] 
雑誌『TIME』やベストセラーの翻訳も手掛け、英語界でその名を馳せる実力講師。

大岩 秀樹 先生 [英語]
情熱あふれる授業で、知らず知らずのうちに英語が得意教科に!

武藤 一也 先生 [英語]
国際的な英語資格(CELTA)に、全世界の上位5%(Pass A)で合格した世界基準の英語講師。

慎 一之 先生 [英語]
関西の実力講師が、全国の東進生に「わかる」感動を伝授。

数学

志田 晶 先生 [数学] 
数学を本質から理解できる本格派講義の完成度は群を抜く。

松田 聡平 先生 [数学]
「ワカル」を「デキル」に変える新しい数学は、君の思考力を刺激し、数学のイメージを覆す!

河合 正人 先生 [数学]
予備校界を代表する講師による魔法のような感動講義を東進で!

沖田 一希 先生 [数学] 
短期間で数学力を徹底的に養成、知識を統一・体系化する!

付録 1

WEBで体験

東進ドットコムで授業を体験できます！
実力講師陣の詳しい紹介や、各教科の学習アドバイスも読めます。
www.toshin.com/teacher/

国語

輿水 淳一先生 [現代文]
「脱・字面読み」トレーニングで、「読む力」を根本から改革する！

西原 剛先生 [現代文]
明快な構造板書と豊富な具体例で必ず君を納得させる！「本物」を伝える現代文の新鋭。

栗原 隆先生 [古文]
東大・難関大志望者から絶大なる信頼を得る本質の指導を追究。

富井 健二先生 [古文]
ビジュアル解説で古文を簡単明快に解き明かす実力講師。

三羽 邦美先生 [古文・漢文]
縦横無尽な知識に裏打ちされた立体的な授業に、グングン引き込まれる！

寺師 貴憲先生 [漢文]
幅広い教養と明解な具体例を駆使した緩急自在の講義。漢文が身近になる！

石関 直子先生 [小論文]
文章で自分を表現できれば、受験も人生も成功できます。「笑顔と努力」で合格を！

理科

宮内 舞子先生 [物理]
丁寧で色彩豊かな板書と詳しい講義で生徒を惹きつける。

鎌田 真彰先生 [化学]
化学現象の基本を疑い化学全体を見通す"伝説の講義"

立脇 香奈先生 [化学]
明朗快活な楽しい講義で、必ず「化学」が好きになる。

田部 眞哉先生 [生物]
全国の受験生が絶賛するその授業は、わかりやすさそのもの！

地歴公民

金谷 俊一郎先生 [日本史]
入試頻出事項に的を絞った「表解板書」は圧倒的な信頼を得る。

井之上 勇先生 [日本史]
つねに生徒と同じ目線に立って、入試問題に対する的確な思考法を教えてくれる。

荒巻 豊志先生 [世界史]
"受験世界史に荒巻あり"といわれる超実力人気講師。

加藤 和樹先生 [世界史]
世界史を「暗記」科目だなんて言わせない。正しく理解すれば必ず伸びることを一緒に体感しよう。

山岡 信幸先生 [地理]
わかりやすい図解と統計の説明に定評。

清水 雅博先生 [公民]
政治と経済のメカニズムを論理的に解明しながら、入試頻出ポイントを明確に示す。

執行 康弘先生 [公民]
「今」を知ることは「未来」の扉を開くこと。受験に留まらず、目標を高く、そして強く持て！

付録 **2**

合格の秘訣 2　基礎から志望校対策まで合格に必要なすべてを網羅した　学習システム

映像によるIT授業を駆使した最先端の勉強法

高速学習

一人ひとりの
レベル・目標にぴったりの授業

東進はすべての授業を映像化しています。その数およそ1万種類。これらの授業を個別に受講できるので、一人ひとりのレベル・目標に合った学習が可能です。1.5倍速受講ができるほか自宅からも受講できるので、今までにない効率的な学習が実現します。

現役合格者の声

東京大学 理科一類
大宮 拓朝くん
東京都立 武蔵高校卒

得意な科目は高2のうちに入試範囲を修了したり、苦手な科目を集中的に取り組んだり、自分の状況に合わせて早め早めの対策ができました。林修先生をはじめ、実力講師陣の授業はおススメです。

1年分の授業を
最短2週間から1カ月で受講

従来の予備校は、毎週1回の授業。一方、東進の高速学習なら毎日受講することができます。だから、1年分の授業も最短2週間から1カ月程度で修了可能。先取り学習や苦手科目の克服、勉強と部活との両立も実現できます。

先取りカリキュラム

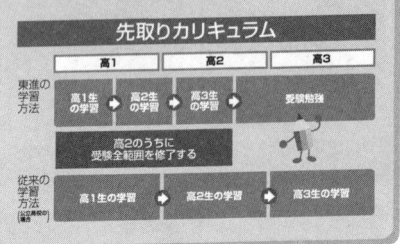

	高1	高2	高3
東進の学習方法	高1生の学習 → 高2生の学習 → 高3生の学習		受験勉強
	高2のうちに受験全範囲を修了する		
従来の学習方法（一般的な予備校の場合）	高1生の学習 → 高2生の学習 → 高3生の学習		

目標まで一歩ずつ確実に

スモールステップ・
パーフェクトマスター

自分にぴったりのレベルから学べる
習ったことを確実に身につける

高校入門から最難関大までの12段階から自分に合ったレベルを選ぶことが可能です。「簡単すぎる」「難しすぎる」といったことがなく、志望校へ最短距離で進みます。
授業後すぐに確認テストを行い内容が身についたかを確認し、合格したら次の授業に進むので、わからない部分を残すことはありません。短期集中で徹底理解をくり返し、学力を高めます。

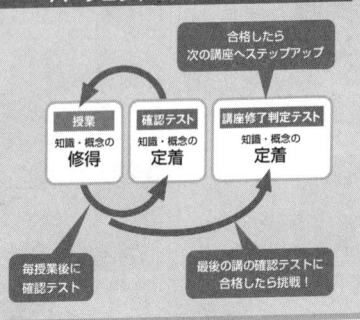

現役合格者の声

一橋大学 商学部
伊原 雪乃さん
千葉県 私立 市川高校卒

高1の「共通テスト同日体験受験」をきっかけに東進に入学しました。毎回の授業後に「確認テスト」があるおかげで、授業に自然と集中して取り組むことができました。コツコツ勉強を続けることが大切です。

パーフェクトマスターのしくみ

合格したら次の講座へステップアップ

授業（知識・概念の**修得**）→ 確認テスト（知識・概念の**定着**）→ 講座修了判定テスト（知識・概念の**定着**）

毎授業後に確認テスト

最後の講の確認テストに合格したら挑戦！

付録 3

| 東進で勉強したいけど、近くに校舎がない君は… | **東進ハイスクール 在宅受講コースへ** | 「遠くて東進の校舎に通えない……」。そんな君も大丈夫！ 在宅受講コースなら自宅のパソコンを使って勉強できます。ご希望の方には、在宅受講コースのパンフレットをお送りいたします。お電話にてご連絡ください。学習・進路相談も随時可能です。 | **0120-531-104** |

徹底的に学力の土台を固める

高速マスター基礎力養成講座

高速マスター基礎力養成講座は「知識」と「トレーニング」の両面から、効率的に短期間で基礎学力を徹底的に身につけるための講座です。英単語をはじめとして、数学や国語の基礎項目も効率よく学習できます。オンラインで利用できるため、校舎だけでなく、スマートフォンアプリで学習することも可能です。

現役合格者の声

早稲田大学 法学部
小松 朋生くん
埼玉県立 川越高校卒

サッカー部と両立しながら志望校に合格できました。それは「高速マスター基礎力養成講座」に全力で取り組んだおかげだと思っています。スキマ時間でも、机に座って集中してでもできるおススメのコンテンツです。

東進公式スマートフォンアプリ
東進式マスター登場！
(英単語／英熟語／英文法／基本例文)

スマートフォンアプリでスキマ時間も徹底活用！

1) スモールステップ・パーフェクトマスター！
頻出度（重要度）の高い英単語から始め、1つのSTAGE（計100語）を完全修得すると次のSTAGEに進めるようになります。

2) 自分の英語力が一目でわかる！
トップ画面に「修得語数・修得率」をメーター表示。自分が今何語修得しているのか、どこを優先的に学習すべきなのか一目でわかります。

3)「覚えていない単語」だけを集中攻略できる！
未修得の単語、または「My単語（自分でチェック登録した単語）」だけをテストする出題設定が可能です。
すでに覚えている単語を何度も学習するような無駄を省き、効率良く単語力を高めることができます。

- 共通テスト対応 英単語1800
- 共通テスト対応 英熟語750
- 英文法750
- 英語基本例文300

「共通テスト対応英単語1800」2022年共通テストカバー率99.5%！

君の合格力を徹底的に高める

志望校対策

第一志望校突破のために、志望校対策にどこよりもこだわり、合格力を徹底的に極める質・量ともに抜群の学習システムを提供します。従来からの「過去問演習講座」に加え、AIを活用した「志望校別単元ジャンル演習講座」、「第一志望校対策演習講座」で合格力を飛躍的に高めます。東進が持つ大学受験に関するビッグデータをもとに、個別対応の演習プログラムを実現しました。限られた時間の中で、君の得点力を最大化します。

現役合格者の声

東京工業大学 環境・社会理工学院
小林 杏彩さん
東京都 私立 豊島岡女子学園高校卒

志望校を高1の頃から決めていて、高3の夏以降は目標をしっかり持って「過去問演習」、「志望校別単元ジャンル演習講座」を進めていきました。苦手教科を克服するのに役立ちました。

大学受験に必須の演習
過去問演習講座

1. 最大10年分の徹底演習
2. 厳正な採点、添削指導
3. 5日以内のスピード返却
4. 再添削指導で着実に得点力強化
5. 実力講師陣による解説授業

東進×AIでかつてない志望校対策
志望校別単元ジャンル演習講座

過去問演習講座の実施状況や、東進模試の結果など、東進で活用したすべての学習履歴をAIが総合的に分析。学習の優先順位をつけ、志望校別に「必勝必達演習セット」として十分な演習問題を提供します。問題は東進が分析した、大学入試問題の膨大なデータベースから提供されます。苦手を克服し、一人ひとりに適切な志望校対策を実現する日本初の学習システムです。

志望校合格に向けた最後の切り札
第一志望校対策演習講座

第一志望校の総合演習に特化した、大学が求める解答力を身につけていきます。対応大学は校舎にお問い合わせください。

付録 **4**

合格の秘訣3 東進模試

申込受付中
※お問い合わせ先は付録7ページをご覧ください。

学力を伸ばす模試

■ 本番を想定した「厳正実施」
統一実施日の「厳正実施」で、実際の入試と同じレベル・形式・試験範囲の「本番レベル」模試。相対評価に加え、絶対評価で学力の伸びを具体的な点数で把握できます。

■ 12大学のべ35回の「大学別模試」の実施
予備校界随一のラインアップで志望校に特化した"学力の精密検査"として活用できます（同日体験受験を含む）。

■ 単元・ジャンル別の学力分析
対策すべき単元・ジャンルを一覧で明示。学習の優先順位がつけられます。

■ 中5日で成績表返却
WEBでは最短で3日で成績を確認できます。
※マーク式の模試のみ

■ 合格指導解説授業
模試受験後に合格指導解説授業を実施。重要ポイントが手に取るようにわかります。

東進模試 ラインアップ 2022年度

模試名	対象	回数
共通テスト本番レベル模試	受験生 高2生 高1生 ※高1は難関大志望者	年4回
高校レベル記述模試	高2生 高1生	年2回
全国統一高校生テスト ●問題は学年別	高3生 高2生 高1生	年2回
全国統一中学生テスト ●問題は学年別	中3生 中2生 中1生	年2回
早慶上理・難関国公立大模試	受験生	年5回
全国有名国公私大模試	受験生	年5回
東大本番レベル模試	受験生	各年4回
高2東大本番レベル模試	高2生 高1生	各年4回

※共通テスト本番レベル模試との総合評価※

模試名	対象	回数
京大本番レベル模試	受験生	年4回
北大本番レベル模試	受験生	年2回
東北大本番レベル模試	受験生	年2回
名大本番レベル模試	受験生	年3回
阪大本番レベル模試	受験生	年3回
九大本番レベル模試	受験生	年3回
東工大本番レベル模試	受験生	年2回
一橋大本番レベル模試	受験生	年2回
千葉大本番レベル模試	受験生	年1回
神戸大本番レベル模試	受験生	年1回
広島大本番レベル模試	受験生	年1回
大学合格基礎力判定テスト	受験生 高2生 高1生	年4回
共通テスト同日体験受験	高2生 高1生	年1回
東大入試同日体験受験	高2生 高1生 ※高1は意欲ある東大志望者	年1回
東北大入試同日体験受験	高2生 高1生 ※高1は意欲ある東北大志望者	年1回
名大入試同日体験受験	高2生 高1生 ※高1は意欲ある名大志望者	年1回
医学部82大学判定テスト	受験生	年2回
中学学力判定テスト	中2生 中1生	年4回

※ 最終回が共通テスト後の受験となる模試は、共通テスト自己採点との総合判定となります。
※ 2022年度に実施予定の模試は、今後の状況により変更する場合があります。
最新の情報はホームページでご確認ください。

2022年東進生大勝利!
東大・難関大 現役合格 史上最高! 連続

東大 現役合格 日本一!※1 853名
昨対 +37名

- 文科一類 138名
- 文科二類 111名
- 文科三類 105名
- 理科一類 310名
- 理科二類 120名
- 理科三類 36名
- 学校推薦 33名

※1 東大現役合格者数はホームページ・パンフレット・チラシ等で公表している29の学習塾・予備校の2022年入試の比較。

現役合格者の38.0%が東進生! 東進生現役占有率 38.0%

※2 2022年の東大全体の現役合格者は2,241名。東進の現役合格者は853名。東進生の占有率は38.0%。現役合格者の2.7人に1人が東進生です。

史上最高!

学校推薦型選抜も東進! **33名/86名** 昨対+10名
現役推薦合格者の38.3%が東進生!
38% 33%
'20 '22 史上最高!

東進史上最高記録を更新!!
'20 802名 '21 816名 '22 853名
現役生のみ! 講習生含まず!

国公立医・医 1,032名 昨対+45名

現役合格者の 29.6%が東進生!

2022年の国公立医学部医学科全体の現役合格者は公表のため、仮に昨年の現役合格者数（推定）3,478名を分母として東進生占有率を計算すると、東進生の占有率は29.6%。現役合格者の3.4人に1人が東進生です。

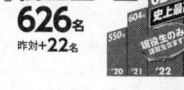

東進生現役占有率 29.6%
'20 825名 '21 987名 '22 1,032名 史上最高!

旧七帝大 +東工大・一橋大・神戸大 4,612名 昨対+246名

- 東京大 853名
- 京都大 468名
- 北海道大 438名
- 東北大 372名
- 名古屋大 410名
- 大阪大 617名
- 九州大 437名
- 東京工業大 211名
- 一橋大 251名
- 神戸大 555名

'20 4,118名 '21 4,366名 '22 4,612名 史上最高!

早慶 5,678名 昨対+485名

- 早稲田大 3,412名
- 慶應義塾大 2,266名

'20 4,636名 '21 5,193名 '22 5,678名 史上最高!

上理明青立法中 21,321名 昨対+2,637名

- 上智大 1,488名
- 東京理科大 2,805名
- 明治大 5,351名
- 青山学院大 2,111名
- 立教大 2,646名
- 法政大 3,848名
- 中央大 3,072名

史上最高!

関関同立 12,633名 昨対+832名

- 関西学院大 2,621名
- 関西大 2,752名
- 同志社大 2,806名
- 立命館大 4,454名

史上最高!

私立医・医 626名 昨対+22名

'20 550名 '21 604名 '22 626名

日東駒専 10,011名 史上最高! 昨対+917名

産近甲龍 6,085名 史上最高! 昨対+368名

国公立大 16,502名 昨対+68名

'20 16,431名 '21 16,434名 '22 16,502名 史上最高!

国公立 総合・学校推薦型選抜も東進!

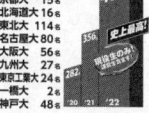

国公立医・医 302名 昨対+15名
'20 267名 '21 287名 '22 302名 史上最高!

旧七帝大+東工大・一橋大・神戸大 415名 昨対+59名

- 東京大 33名
- 京都大 15名
- 北海道大 16名
- 東北大 114名
- 名古屋大 80名
- 大阪大 56名
- 九州大 27名
- 東京工業大 24名
- 一橋大 2名
- 神戸大 48名

'20 339名 '21 356名 '22 415名 史上最高!

ウェブサイトでもっと詳しく
東進　🔍検索

2022年3月31日締切　付録 6

各大学の合格実績は、東進ネットワーク（東進ハイスクール、東進衛星予備校、早稲田塾）の現役生のみ、高3時在籍者のみの合同実績です。一人で複数合格した場合は、それぞれの合格者数に計上しています。

東進へのお問い合わせ・資料請求は
東進ドットコム www.toshin.com
もしくは下記のフリーコールへ！

ハッキリ言って合格実績が自慢です！ 大学受験なら、
東進ハイスクール　0120-104-555（トーシン ゴーゴーゴー）

●東京都
[中央地区]
校舎	電話番号
□市ヶ谷校	0120-104-205
□新宿エルタワー校	0120-104-121
＊新宿校大学受験本科	0120-104-020
高田馬場校	0120-104-770
人形町校	0120-104-075

[城北地区]
校舎	電話番号
赤羽校	0120-104-293
本郷三丁目校	0120-104-068
茗荷谷校	0120-738-104

[城東地区]
校舎	電話番号
綾瀬校	0120-104-762
金町校	0120-452-104
亀戸校	0120-104-889
□★北千住校	0120-693-104
錦糸町校	0120-104-249
豊洲校	0120-104-282
西新井校	0120-266-104
西葛西校	0120-289-104
船堀校	0120-104-201
門前仲町校	0120-104-016

[城西地区]
校舎	電話番号
池袋校	0120-104-062
大泉学園校	0120-104-862
荻窪校	0120-687-104
高円寺校	0120-104-627
石神井校	0120-104-159
巣鴨校	0120-104-780
成増校	0120-028-104
練馬校	0120-104-643

[城南地区]
校舎	電話番号
大井町校	0120-575-104
蒲田校	0120-265-104
五反田校	0120-672-104
三軒茶屋校	0120-104-739
渋谷駅西口校	0120-389-104
下北沢校	0120-104-672
自由が丘校	0120-964-104
成城学園前駅北口校	0120-104-616
千歳烏山校	0120-104-331
千歳船橋校	0120-104-825
都立大学駅前校	0120-275-104
中目黒校	0120-104-261
二子玉川校	0120-104-959

[東京都下]
校舎	電話番号
吉祥寺校	0120-104-775
国立校	0120-104-599
国分寺校	0120-622-104
立川駅北口校	0120-104-662
田無校	0120-104-272
調布校	0120-104-305
八王子校	0120-896-104
東久留米校	0120-565-104
府中校	0120-104-676
□★町田校	0120-104-507
三鷹校	0120-104-149
武蔵小金井校	0120-480-104
武蔵境校	0120-104-769

●神奈川県
青葉台校	0120-104-947
厚木校	0120-104-716
川崎校	0120-226-104
湘南台東口校	0120-104-706
新百合ヶ丘校	0120-104-182
センター南駅前校	0120-104-722
たまプラーザ校	0120-104-445
鶴見校	0120-876-104
登戸校	0120-104-157
平塚校	0120-104-742
藤沢校	0120-104-549
□武蔵小杉校	0120-165-104
★横浜校	0120-104-473

●埼玉県
□浦和校	0120-104-561
□大宮校	0120-104-858
春日部校	0120-104-508
川口校	0120-917-104
川越校	0120-104-538
小手指校	0120-104-759
志木校	0120-104-202
せんげん台校	0120-104-388
草加校	0120-104-690
所沢校	0120-104-594
★南浦和校	0120-104-573
与野校	0120-104-755

●千葉県
我孫子校	0120-104-253
市川駅前校	0120-104-381
稲毛海岸校	0120-104-575
海浜幕張校	0120-104-926
□★柏校	0120-104-353
北習志野校	0120-344-104
□新浦安校	0120-556-104
新松戸校	0120-104-354
□千葉校	0120-104-564
□★津田沼校	0120-104-724
成田駅前校	0120-104-346
船橋校	0120-104-514
松戸校	0120-104-257
南柏校	0120-104-439
八千代台校	0120-104-863

●茨城県
つくば校	0120-403-104
取手校	0120-104-328

●静岡県
□★静岡校	0120-104-585

●長野県
校舎	電話番号
□★長野校	0120-104-586

●奈良県
□★奈良校	0120-104-597

★は高卒本科(高卒生)設置校
＊は高卒生専用校舎
□は中学部設置校

※変更の可能性があります。
最新情報はウェブサイトで確認できます。

全国約1,000校、10万人の高校生が通う、
東進衛星予備校　0120-104-531（トーシン ゴーサイン）

東進ドットコム　www.toshin.com
ここでしか見られない受験と教育の最新情報が満載！
[東進] 検索

大学案内
最新の入試に対応した大学情報をまとめて掲載。偏差値ランキングもこちらから！

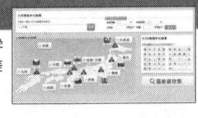

大学入試過去問データベース
君が目指す大学の過去問を素早く検索できる！2022年入試の過去問も閲覧可能！
185大学 最大28年分を無料で提供！

東進TV
東進のYouTube公式チャンネル「東進TV」。日本全国の学生レポーターがお送りする大学・学部紹介は必見！

東進WEB書店
ベストセラー参考書から、夢膨らむ人生の参考書まで、君の学びをバックアップ！

付録 7

※2022年4月現在